COMPREHENSIVE RESEARCH
AND STUDY GUIDE

Edgar Allan Poe

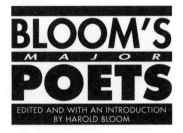

EDITED AND WITH AN INTRODUCTION
BY HAROLD BLOOM

CURRENTLY AVAILABLE

BLOOM'S MAJOR WORLD POETS

Geoffrey Chaucer

Emily Dickinson

John Donne

T. S. Eliot

Robert Frost

Langston Hughes

John Milton

Edgar Allan Poe

Shakespeare's Poems & Sonnets

Alfred, Lord Tennyson

Walt Whitman

William Wordsworth

BLOOM'S MAJOR SHORT STORY WRITERS

William Faulkner

F. Scott Fitzgerald

Ernest Hemingway

O. Henry

James Joyce

Herman Melville

Flannery O'Connor

Edgar Allan Poe

J. D. Salinger

John Steinbeck

Mark Twain

Eudora Welty

COMPREHENSIVE RESEARCH
AND STUDY GUIDE

Edgar Allan Poe

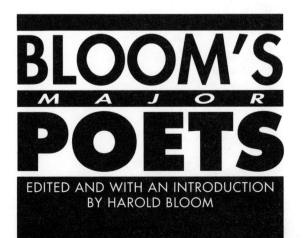

BLOOM'S
M A J O R
POETS

EDITED AND WITH AN INTRODUCTION
BY HAROLD BLOOM

3 5 7 9 8 6 4 2

Library of Congress Cataloging-in-Publication Data

Edgar Allan Poe / edited and with an introduction by Harold Bloom.
cm. – (Bloom's major poets)
Includes bibliographical references and index.
ISBN 0-7910-5113-7
Poe, Edgar Allan, 1809-1849—Poetic works—Handbooks, manuals,
Etc.   2. Poe, Edgar Allan, 1809-1849—Poetic works—Examinations—
Study guides.   3. Fantasy poetry, American—History and criticism—
Examinations—Study guides.   I. Bloom, Harold.   II. Series.
PS2643.P63E34   1998
818'.309—dc21
98-43450
CIP

Chelsea House Publishers
1974 Sproul Road, Suite 400
Broomall, PA 19008-091

Contributing Editor: Barbara Fischer

Contents

User's Guide

This volume is designed to present biographical, critical, and bibliographical information on the author's best-known or most important poems. Following Harold Bloom's editor's note and introduction is a detailed biography of the author, discussing major life events and important literary accomplishments. A thematic and structural analysis of each poem follows, tracing significant themes, patterns, and motifs in the work.

A selection of critical extracts, derived from previously published material from leading critics, analyzes aspects of each poem. The extracts consist of statements from the author, if available, early reviews of the work, and later evaluations up to the present. A bibliography of the author's writings (including a complete list of all books written, cowritten, edited, and translated), a list of additional books and articles on the author and the work, and an index of themes and ideas in the author's writings conclude the volume.

~

Harold Bloom is Sterling Professor of the Humanities at Yale University and Henry W. and Albert A. Berg Professor of English at the New York University Graduate School. He is the author of over 20 books and the editor of more than 30 anthologies of literary criticism.

Professor Bloom's works include *Shelley's Mythmaking* (1959), *The Visionary Company* (1961), *Blake's Apocalypse* (1963), *Yeats* (1970), *A Map of Misreading* (1975), *Kabbalah and Criticism* (1975), and *Agon: Toward a Theory of Revisionism* (1982). *The Anxiety of Influence* (1973) sets forth Professor Bloom's provocative theory of the literary relationships between the great writers and their predecessors. His most recent books include *The American Religion* (1992), *The Western Canon* (1994), *Omens of Millennium: The Gnosis of Angels, Dreams, and Resurrection* (1996), and *Shakespeare: The Invention of the Human* (1998).

Professor Bloom earned his Ph.D. from Yale University in 1955 and has served on the Yale faculty since then. He is a 1985 MacArthur Foundation Award recipient and served as the Charles Eliot Norton Professor of Poetry at Harvard University in 1987–88. He is currently the editor of other Chelsea House series in literary criticism, including BLOOM'S NOTES, BLOOM'S MAJOR SHORT STORY WRITERS, MAJOR LITERARY CHARACTERS, MODERN CRITICAL VIEWS, MODERN CRITICAL INTERPRETATIONS, and WOMEN WRITERS OF ENGLISH AND THEIR WORKS.

Editor's Note

My Introduction laments the aesthetic inadequacy of Poe's poetry, while conceding that this does not at all inhibit its permanent popularity.

There are copious Critical Views excerpted in this volume, so that I will comment upon only a few high points. Yvor Winters, who wrongly accused many other American writers of obscurantism, is accurate in censoring Poe.

Richard Wilbur, an American poet of the greatest distinction, defends Poe as a master of the realm of dreams. "The City in the Sea" is very usefully studied by Douglas Novich Leonard and by J. Lasley Dameron, while Joan Dayan sees Poe as a strategist of poetic language.

D. H. Lawrence, to me Poe's best critic, reflects upon Roderick Usher and "The Haunted Palace," while T. S. Eliot, true to French tradition, sees Poe through the eyes of the Symbolists.

John T. Irwin, Lawrence's only rival on Poe, restores Poe's sense of "infinity," after which Grover Smith speculates on Poe's influence in regard to Eliot.

W. H. Auden discusses Poe's formal limitations in "The Raven," while Debra Fried brilliantly notes that repetition, in the poem, "is quite explicitly death." Perhaps that is another clue to the enigmas of Poe's worldwide popularity; his hypnotic repetitions arouse our own apprehension of what Hamlet called "that undiscovered country."

Introduction

HAROLD BLOOM

Poe is the largest puzzle in American poetry. His most celebrated poems are jingles: "The Raven," "The Bells," "Annabel Lee," and the ghastly "Ulalume." When he is somewhat better, his precursors Byron, Coleridge, and Shelley always hover too closely. But Poe is as inescapable in his bad verses as he is in his badly written tales, which are nightmares of diction as well as of vision. Baudelaire, Mallarme, and Valery all adored Poe's poetry, but then their ears were not well attuned to English as a language. Poe's tales survive, and evidently will be popular reading forever. Poetry is less widely read, yet Poe's verse must have a larger audience than any other American poet, including Whitman and Frost. This may be beyond explanation; I open Poe's *Poetry* completely at random, and read:

> For the heart whose woes are legion
> 'Tis a peaceful, soothing region—

This is from "Dream-Land"; its observation is neither true nor interesting, and the rhyme is dreadful. "Legions of regions," one wants to chant, or is it: "Regions of legions"? Anyone who thinks that Poe was a great poet should be asked to recite "For Annie" out loud:

> Sadly, I know
>   I am shorn of my strength,
> And no muscle I move
>   As I lie at full length—
> But no matter! — I feel
>   I am better at length.

The enigma of Poe's survival clearly is explained by his universality. I myself was rather startled some fifteen years ago, when I published a review-essay that emphasized both Poe's hysterical badness and his inescapability, by the avalanche of protests I called up. Letters poured in, many questioning my motives, and at least two radio programs accommodated outraged lovers of Poe, some of them quite passionate at denouncing me. Poe can write as badly as anyone in the language, but it makes little difference. Legions of many regions (not just the South) charge fiercely in his favor, with quasi-religious zeal. The cultural effect and influence of Poe transcend his aesthetic inadequacies. As a literary critic with little use for what is now termed "cultural criticism," I tend to believe that Poe's bad eminence relies upon the popular taste for repetition, easy tunes, and exacerbated intensity, indeed for hysteria as such. Since Poe had the singular genius to incarnate and express a peculiarly American hysteria, we shall never be done with him. ❀

Biography of
Edgar Allan Poe

(1809–1849)

Best known for his short stories, Edgar Allan Poe aspired to write poetry from an early age and considered poetry his highest calling. In the preface to *The Raven and Other Poems* (1845), Poe explains, "Events not to be controlled have prevented me from making, at any time, any serious effort in what, under happier circumstances, would have been the field of my choice. With me poetry has been not a purpose, but a passion . . . ." He left behind a strangely dual legacy: he wrote a few of the most famous and best-remembered poems in American history, and critics continue to judge him to be a lousy poet. Dismissed as a songster or "jingle man" in his own day, a hundred years later his "jingles" were still being read, and critic Yvor Winters forcefully dismissed him as a "bad writer accidentally and temporarily popular." Though the literary quality of Poe's poetry remains a disputed matter, the charge of "temporary" popularity can certainly be refuted. Poe's poems remain memorable for their evocation of nightmarish scenes, desolate wastes, and tragic passions: as Harold Bloom has pointed out, "Poe was and is our hysteria."

To find a source for that hysteria in Poe's life does not require much imagination. Poe was born in Boston on January 19, 1809, to actors David and Elizabeth Arnold Poe. Poe's father deserted the family when Poe was an infant. At age three, Poe witnessed his mother's death, watching as she died coughing up blood from tuberculosis after a performance. Poe was then raised by foster parents Frances and John Allan, who educated him in private academies in England and Virginia. The young Poe demonstrated precocious poetic ability, and his foster father considered publishing the eleven-year-old's manuscript of poems, but decided against flattering the boy's vanity.

In 1826, Poe entered the University of Virginia. After quarrelling with John Allan, who refused to pay the $2000 gambling debt Poe had incurred, he fled to Boston and joined the army. While there, he published *Tamerlane and Other Poems* (1827) "by a Bostonian," but the volume went unnoticed. He considered a professional military career and gained admission to West Point with John Allan's help. Relations with his foster father remained tense, however, especially after the death of Frances Allan, for whom Poe had strong affections. Allan, who never officially adopted him, refused to subsidize a second volume of poems, but Poe, living with relatives in Baltimore, managed to publish *Al Aaraaf, Tamerlane and Minor Poems* (1829) to brief critical approval.

Popular at West Point for his satires on cadet life, Poe continued to struggle for financial security, his situation made more dire after John Allan remarried and severed relations with him. Managing to raise money from his classmates, Poe published *Poems* (1831) and then promptly got himself expelled from the academy. He returned to Baltimore to live with his paternal aunt, Maria Clemm, and her daughter Virginia, and began writing short stories and reviews to pay the bills. He gained a reputation as a learned but harsh critic writing for the *Southern Literary Messenger,* where he was eventually hired as an editor.

In 1836, Poe married his not quite fourteen-year-old cousin Virginia. A marriage of convenience that was perhaps unconsummated, it offered Poe both an idealized love object and a semblance of domestic stability. Moving from city to city in this household of aunt, nephew, and child-bride, Poe continued to grapple with a tortured and anxiety-ridden emotional as well as professional life. Prone to despair, alcoholism, and conflicts with authority, Poe was dismissed from the *Messenger* and sought employment in New York and Philadelphia. He pieced together a living through hack work, selling cryptograms and various features. He also began to publish stories that gained him a growing readership and a literary reputation, including "The Fall of the House of Usher" in *Burton's Gentleman's Magazine* in 1839. Late in that year, he published a volume of 25 stories entitled *Tales of the Grotesque and Arabesque.*

In 1841 he became a well-salaried editor of *Graham's Magazine,* to which he contributed his first "tales of ratiocination," including "The Murders in the Rue Morgue," the story that marks the invention of the detective story. Professional success was marred by personal tragedy in 1842, however, as Virginia suffered a ruptured blood vessel in her throat while singing, a near fatal illness from which she never fully recovered. In this period, Poe wrote some of his finest stories and continued his efforts to launch a literary magazine of his own. His drunkenness ruined chances for stable employment, but he nonetheless gained fame as writer of tales, his popularity enhanced by a phony account of a trans-Atlantic balloon flight.

In a triumphant and opportunistic return to poetry in 1845, Poe published "The Raven." The poem was an instant hit, leading to the publication of *The Raven and Other Poems*, critical acclaim, and a lecture tour. But with Virginia's health deteriorating and his own mental, physical, and financial well-being precarious, Poe was unable to function in a normal social capacity. Already notorious for his debauchery and erratic behavior, he was plunged into severe depression after Virginia's death from tuberculosis in 1847.

Poe appeared to be improving in health and maintaining sobriety the following year, and wrote *Eureka,* his prose-poem "On the Material and Spiritual Universe." He engaged in several "literary courtships" with married and unmarried women, including Sarah Helen Whitman, whose refusal of his offer of marriage reportedly induced him to attempt suicide with an overdose of laudanum.

In 1848, Poe read "The Poetic Principle" as a lecture in Providence, putting forth some of his most influential views on poetry as "the rhythmical creation of beauty." His emphasis on pleasure, not instruction, as the purpose of poetry, and his rejection of intellectual content in favor of musicality and supernal beauty, greatly influenced the French Symbolists, who took Poe as a poetic icon. Many poets and critics consider the high praise that Baudelaire, Mallarmé, and Valéry had for Poe's aesthetic theories to be an overvaluation.

Despite his attempts to control his alcoholism, Poe continued to relapse, suffering from physical illnesses, anxiety, and a persecution complex. He was found delirious in Baltimore, where he died on October 7, 1849. Rufus Griswold, Poe's literary executor, published a slanderous obituary that damaged Poe's reputation, and the portrayal of Poe as an opium fiend persists today despite attempts to redress exaggerations. A figure of tragic melancholy, both condemned and embraced for his degraded, despairing, and tempestuous life, Poe as poet continues to haunt the imaginations of readers as strongly as the incantatory rhythms of his poems. ❀

Thematic Analysis of
"The City in the Sea"

First published as "The Doomed City" in *Poems* (1831) and reprinted with minor revisions as "The City of Sin" in 1836, "The City in the Sea" appeared in *The Raven and Other Poems* (1845). In the final version, Poe omits the concluding couplet "And Death to some happy clime / Shall give his undivided time," ending the poem more sharply with the image of the sinking city revered by Hell itself. Several critics consider the poem to be Poe's best, praising its nebulous and phantasmagoric imagery. Poe states perhaps too explicitly that the scene is intended to evoke melancholy resignation, drawing our attention to "gaping graves," an image that has become a quintessential "Poe-esque" figure for death-obsession. When the poem sounds at times conventional in its morbid gloom, we are responding in part to our familiarity with conventions that Poe himself inaugurated in American poetry. Without making any statement of human tragedy, and with oddly ambiguous lavishness, Poe weaves a sense of doom, cold finality, and spiritual vacuity.

Poe's lost city "Far down within the dim West" suggests several sources, including the legendary Atlantis, a large island in the Western ocean, beyond the straits of Gibraltar, that Plato had described as a paradise destroyed by earthquake. Poe's city also reflects accounts of the biblical city of Gomorrah, condemned by God for its sins and buried in the Dead Sea. With the description of the city's "Babylon-like walls," Poe also invites comparison with an ancient city of splendor, luxury, and corruption (the traditional symbolism of Babylon found in biblical passages, such as Isaiah 14:4–23 and Revelation 16:18–19). Inspired by these ideas about condemned cities, the poem presents the desolate landscape of a world frozen in a post-apocalyptic state.

Poe found inspiration in more recent sources as well. He was strongly influenced by the English Romantic poets, especially John Keats (1795–1821), George Gordon, Lord Byron (1788–1824), and Samuel Taylor Coleridge (1772–1834), whose aesthetic theories in *Biographia Literaria* (1817) form the underpinnings of many of Poe's own views. "The City in the Sea" reflects the particular influence of Byron's poem "Darkness" (1816), which relates the horror of a world in which "the bright sun was extinguish'd." Poe's poem echoes Byron's theme and his diction. In Poe, "Death has reared himself a throne / In a strange city lying alone"; in Byron, the annihilated waste reduces civilization until "All earth was but one thought—and that was death . . . ." The utter stillness of Poe's city, with its "time-eaten towers that tremble not" and waters where "no ripples curl," reflects Byron's description of a scene where "The rivers, lakes, and ocean all stood still, / And nothing stirred within their silent depths." Poe's open graves "yawn level with the luminous waves"; Byron's ships rot on the sea because even "the tides were in their grave."

Poe's extensive borrowings have led several critics to label his effort as simply derivative, but he brings to the scene a strange illumination all his own. The panorama is otherworldly: its "shrines and palaces and towers / . . . / Resemble nothing that is ours." Poe negates the city's connection to the known human world and also refuses the possibility that metaphor might create a "resemblance." The city's architecture is weirdly lit from beneath by "light from out the lurid sea," light that "streams up the turrets" from the bottom. Human constructions—domes, spires, halls, fanes (temples), and walls—have an eerie and chilling aura. The poem has a cinematic quality, as if the observer were watching through a camera panning along undersea wreckage, then zooming in to focus on a smaller artifact. Three symbols of civilization intertwine on "wreathéd friezes": a "viol," representing the fine arts, a "violet" of beauty and cultivation, and a "vine" of human sacrament and communion, as well as revelry. Poe heightens the pathos of the poem by presenting this image of a living culture as irrevocably lost in a strangely lit world. The water that has engulfed the objects then blurs our vision of them: "so blend the turrets and shadows there / That all seems pendulous in air." With this image, Poe telescopes back and presents the scene from an almost Miltonic perspective (Milton had described the "pendant world" in *Paradise Lost* II). Poe reaches for an effect of tremendous scope when he describes the personified "Death" peering down upon the ruined town.

Several critics have puzzled over the difficulty of envisioning the dimensions and perspective of this city "in the sea" (see Leonard, extracted below). Poe's distorted images resist attempts to "diagram" the physical design. More importantly, the thematic and moral significance of the scene remains unclear. Poe presents a vision that invites an allegorical interpretation but then baffles attempts to assign the terms of the allegory. Faced with "gaping graves," the reader becomes aware of human mortality, perhaps even aware of the transience of material wealth. The reader might conclude that Poe suggests that forces of nature will inevitably overwhelm human vanity. The poem does not, however, imply that any moral judgment has taken place. We do not know how or why the city was damned, or by what agency. God is strikingly absent, as Robert Jacobs has pointed out. Yvor Winters argues that the poem is constructed with "all of the paraphernalia of allegory except the significance," leaving the reader with a "feeling of meaning withheld." For some readers a source of frustration, this "withholding" is for others the poem's allure. The vision of complete stasis, of a "wilderness of glass" where the city is crystallized, sharply contrasts the inhabited world. In "some far-off happier sea," change continues to take place, but here "no heavings hint," and all things remain in a "hideously serene," motionless state. Poe does not editorialize on this horrifying paralysis, nor does he name the cause or effect of this doomed world.

With the exclamation that begins the final stanza, we observe a faint suggestion of movement. Over the course of the poem, Poe acutely focuses perception so that we now detect the slightest "stir." We learn that the motion is caused by an upheaval in Hell, which is "rising from a thousand thrones." The city in the sea is so horrible that Hell can appreciate it, even worship it. With the image of a sunset-like "redder glow," Poe suggests that *time*, not space, begins to move: "the hours are breathing faint and low." "No earthly moans" mourn the city's demise, but the supernatural world rises to claim it. Poe's city exists in a strangely abstracted dimension where human judgment, pity, and understanding have been annihilated.

Written in loose tetrameter couplets, the poem relies heavily on alliteration and rhyme to create its melancholy tone. A predominance of long *o* sounds—throne / alone, glow / low, moans / thrones—contributes to the forlorn mood. In the line "the viol, the violet, and the vine," the sonic values of the words themselves entwine as the sculptured motif is said to "intertwine," a musical effect praised by late nineteenth-century poet Ernest Dowson (1867–1900) as creating his favorite line in all poetry. Nonetheless, this same line is cited by Winters as an example of Poe's "resounding puerilities." Whatever the reader's taste, Poe presents highly crafted verses that emphasize the acoustic values of words. As Elizabeth Phillips has observed, the "hissing" of the *s* sounds of the poem's final lines gives the reader a shiver of horror.

Poe's vision of a lost metropolis, its significance displaced by the mesmerizing images and rhythms that draw us into the scene, coolly portrays a world of apocalyptic doom, a world that is "hideous" because it exists in a state of total serenity. The greatest among Poe's early poems, "The City in the Sea" develops themes and stylistic devices that persist in the later poems and tales. Poe sketches a scene where otherworldly dramas seem about to take place, and he will often revisit this dream-scape of loss and isolation. ❀

Critical Views on
"The City in the Sea"

EDGAR ALLAN POE ON "THE POETIC PRINCIPLE"

[Delivered as a lecture in Providence, Rhode Island, in 1848, this summary statement of Poe's aesthetic beliefs defines poetry as "the rhythmical creation of beauty" and describes the poet's "wild effort to reach the Beauty above." Poe argues that the object of poetry is beauty, not truth, denying that poetry should serve a didactic function. This point of view, reflected in the way the "The City in the Sea" is removed from questions of duty or truth, was censured in Poe's day and later, as the extracts below by Walt Whitman and Yvor Winters make clear.]

I allude to the heresy of *The Didactic*. It has been assumed, tacitly and avowedly, directly and indirectly, that the ultimate object of all Poetry is Truth. Every poem, it is said, should inculcate a moral; and by this moral is the poetical merit of the work to be adjudged. We Americans, especially, have developed it in full. We have taken it into our heads that to write a poem simply for the poem's sake, and to acknowledge such to have been our design, would be to confess ourselves radically wanting in the true Poetic dignity and force:—but the simple fact is, that, would we but permit ourselves to look into our own souls, we should immediately there discover that under the sun there neither exists nor *can* exist any work more thoroughly dignified—more supremely noble than this very poem—this poem *per se*—this poem which is a poem and nothing more—this poem written solely for the poem's sake.

With as deep a reverence for the True as ever inspired the bosom of man, I would, nevertheless, limit, in some measure, its modes of inculcation. I would limit to enforce them. I would not enfeeble them by dissipation. The demands of Truth are severe. She has no sympathy with the myrtles. All *that* which is so indispensable in Song, is precisely all *that* with which *she* has nothing whatever to do. It is but making her a flaunting paradox, to wreathe her in gems and flowers. In enforcing a truth, we need severity rather than efflorescence of language. We must be simple, precise, terse. We must be cool, calm, unimpassioned. In a word, we must be in that mood which, as nearly as possible, is the exact converse of the poetical. *He must be blind, indeed, who does not perceive the radical and chasmal differences between the truthful and the poetical modes of inculcation. He* must be theory-mad beyond redemption who, in spite of these differences, shall still persist in attempting to reconcile the obstinate oils and waters of Poetry and Truth. . . .

I would define, in brief, the Poetry of words as *The Rhythmical Creation of Beauty.* Its sole arbiter is Taste. With the Intellect or with the Conscience, it has only collateral relations. Unless incidentally, it has no concern whatever either with Duty or with Truth.

A few words, however, in explanation. *That* pleasure which is at once the most pure, the most elevating, and the most intense, is derived, I maintain, from the contemplation of the Beautiful. In the contemplation of Beauty we alone find it possible to attain that pleasurable elevation, or excitement, *of the soul,* which we recognise as the poetic Sentiment, and which is so easily distinguished from Truth, which is the satisfaction of the Reason, or from Passion, which is the excitement of the heart.

—Edgar Allan Poe, "The Poetic Principle" (1850). Reprinted in *Edgar Allan Poe: Poetry, Tales, & Selected Essays* (New York: Library of America, 1996): pp. 1435–1436, 1438.

☙

WALT WHITMAN ON POE'S CHARACTER

[American poet Walt Whitman (1819–1892), best known for *Leaves of Grass* (1855), had perhaps the single greatest influence on later American poetry. His inclusive and celebratory free verse is at times sensual, egomaniacal, patriotic, elegiac, and incantatory. In this extract, Whitman admires Poe's "intense faculty for technical and abstract beauty," but sees as defects those aspects of Poe's personality that lead to his "strange spurning" of moral principles and to his "nocturnal" and "demoniac" tendencies.]

By common consent there is nothing better for man or woman than a perfect and noble life, morally without flaw, happily balanced in activity, physically sound and pure, giving its due proportion, and no more, to the sympathetic, the human emotional element—a life, in all these, unhasting, unresting, untiring to the end. And yet there is another shape of personality dearer far to the artist-sense, (which likes the play of strongest lights and shades,) where the perfect character, the good, the heroic, although never attain'd, is never lost sight of, but through failures, sorrows, temporary downfalls, is return'd to again and again, and while often violated, is passionately adhered to as long as mind, muscles, voice, obey the power we call volition. This sort of personality we see more or less in Burns, Byron, Schiller, and George Sand. But we do not see it in Edgar Poe. (All this is the result of reading at intervals the last three days a new volume of his poems—I took it on my rambles down by the pond, and by degrees read it all through there.) While to the character first outlined the service Poe renders is certainly that entire contrast and contradiction which is next best to fully exemplifying it.

Almost without the first sign of moral principle, or of the concrete or its heroisms, or the simpler affections of the heart, Poe's verses illustrate an intense faculty for technical and abstract beauty, with the rhyming art to excess, an incorrigible propensity toward nocturnal themes, a demoniac undertone behind every page—and by final judgment, probably belong among the electric lights of imaginative literature, brilliant and dazzling, but with no heat. There is an indescribable magnetism about the poet's life and reminiscences, as well as the poems. To one who could work out their subtle retracing and retrospect, the latter would make a close tally no doubt between the author's birth and antecedents, his childhood and youth, his physique, his so-call'd education, his studies and associates, the literary and social Baltimore, Richmond, Philadelphia and New York of those times—not only the places and circumstances in themselves, but often, very often, in a strange spurning of, and reaction from them all.

—Walt Whitman, *Complete Prose Works* (Philadelphia: D. McKay, 1897): pp. 156–157.

[Yvor Winters (1900–1968), American poet, critic, and long-time professor at Stanford University, was a key figure of the New Criticism. His critical works include *Primitivism and Decadence* (1937), *The Anatomy of Nonsense* (1943), and *The Function of Criticism* (1957). As a general rule, Winters looks for spiritual and moral significance in art. In this essay on Poe's "obscurantism," he criticizes Poe's failure to address "moral truth" and for his treatment of art as "a kind of stimulant, ingeniously concocted."]

Poe's aesthetic is an aesthetic of obscurantism. We have that willful dislocation of feeling from understanding, which, growing out of the uncertainty regarding the nature of moral truth in general and its identity in particular situations which produced such writers as Hawthorne and James, was later to result through the exploitation of special techniques in the violent aberrations of the Experimental School of the twentieth century, culminating in the catastrophe of Hart Crane.

Poe speaks a great deal of the need of originality. This quality, as he understands it, appears to be a fairly simple mechanical device, first, for fixing the attention, and second, for heightening the effect of strangeness. We may obtain a fair idea of his concept of originality of theme from his comment on a poem by Amelia Welby, quoted in the series of brief notes entitled "Minor Contemporaries":

> [. . .] The desire of the new is an element of the soul. The most exquisite pleasures grow dull in repetition. A strain of music enchants. Heard a second time, it pleases. Heard a tenth, it does not displease. We hear it a twentieth, and ask ourselves why we admired. At the fiftieth it produces ennui, at the hundredth disgust.

Now I do not know what music most delighted Poe, unless perchance it may have been the melodies of Thomas Moore, but if I may be permitted to use exact numbers in the same figurative sense in which I conceive that Poe here used them, I am bound to say that my own experience with music differs profoundly. The trouble again is traceable to Poe's failure to understand the moral basis of art, to his view of art as a kind of stimulant, ingeniously concocted, which may, if one is lucky, raise one to a moment of divine delusion. A Bach fugue or a Byrd mass moves us not primarily because of any originality it may display, but because of its sublimity as I have already defined the term. [Winters defines "moral sublimity" as "a sound attitude toward a major problem, communicated with an adequacy of detail."] Rehearing can do no more than give us a fuller and firmer awareness of this quality. The same is true of *Paradise Lost*. Poe fails to see that the originality of a poem lies not in the newness of the general theme—for if it did, the possibilities of poetry would have been exhausted long before the time of Poe—but in the quality of the personal intelligence, as that intelligence appears in the minutiae of style, in the defining limits of thought and of feeling, brought to the subject by the poet who writes of it. The originality, from Poe's point of view, of the subjects of such poems as "The Raven," "The Sleeper," and "Ulalume" would reside in the fantastic dramatic and scenic effects by means of which the subject of simple regret is concealed diffused, and rendered ludicrous. From the same point of view, "Rose Aylmer" would necessarily be lacking in originality.

In "The Philosophy of Composition" Poe gives us a hint as to his conception of originality of style. After a brief discourse on originality of versification, and the unaccountable way in which it has been neglected, he states that he lays no claim to originality as regards the meter or the rhythm of "The Raven," but only as regards the stanza: "nothing even remotely approaching this combination has ever been attempted." Again we see Poe's tendency to rely upon the mechanically startling, in preference to the inimitable. This fact, coupled with his extraordinary theories of meter, which I shall examine separately, bears a close relationship to what appears to me to be the clumsiness and insensitivity of his verse. Read three times, his rhythms disgust, because they are untrained and insensitive and have no individual life within their surprising mechanical frames.

—Yvor Winters, "Edgar Allan Poe: A Crisis in the History of American Obscurantism," *American Literature* 8 (January 1937): pp. 389–391.

[Richard Wilbur has won two Pulitzer prizes (1957 and 1989) and the National Book Award for his poetry, and was the second U.S. poet laureate. He taught at Harvard and Wesleyan, and is also well known as a critic, lyricist, and translator of the French playwrights Molière (1622–1673) and Racine (1639–1699). In this influential essay, Wilbur answers some of the charges of Poe's detractors, arguing for the positive value of his "dark suggestiveness" as evidence of the struggle of a poetic soul not content to use art to give order to earthly experience.]

It is not really surprising that some critics should think Poe meaningless, or that others should suppose his meaning intelligible only to monsters. Poe was not a wide-open and perspicuous writer; indeed, he was a secretive writer both by temperament and by conviction. He sprinkled his stories with sly references to himself and to his personal history. He gave his own birthday of January 19 to his character William Wilson; he bestowed his own height and color of eye on the captain of the phantom ship in *Ms. Found in a Bottle;* and the name of one of his heroes, Arthur Gordon Pym, is patently a version of his own. He was a maker and solver of puzzles, fascinated by codes, ciphers, anagrams, acrostics, hieroglyphics, and the Kabbala. He invented the detective story. He was fond of aliases; he delighted in accounts of swindles; he perpetrated the famous Balloon Hoax of 1844; and one of his most characteristic stories is entitled *Mystification.* A man so devoted to concealment and deception and unraveling and detection might be expected to have in his work what Poe himself called "undercurrents of meaning."

And that is where Poe, as a critic, said that meaning belongs: not on the surface of the poem or tale, but below the surface as a dark undercurrent. If the meaning of a work is made overly clear—as Poe said in his *Philosophy of Composition*—if the meaning is brought to the surface and made the upper current of the poem or tale, then the work becomes bald and prosaic and ceases to be art. Poe conceived of art, you see, not as a means of giving imaginative order to earthly experience, but as a stimulus to unearthly visions. The work of literary art does not, in Poe's view, present the reader with a provisional arrangement of reality; instead, it seeks to disengage the reader's mind from reality and propel it toward the ideal. Now, since Poe thought the function of art was to set the mind soaring upward in what he called "a wild effort to reach the Beauty above," it was important to him that the poem or tale should not have such definiteness and completeness of meaning as might contain the reader's mind within the work. Therefore Poe's criticism places a positive value on the obscuration of meaning, on a dark suggestiveness, on a deliberate vagueness by means of which the reader's mind may be set adrift toward the beyond. [...]

These, then, are Poe's great subjects: first, the war between the poetic soul and the external world; second, the war between the poetic soul and the earthly self to which it is bound. All of Poe's major stories are allegorical presentations of these conflicts, and everything he wrote bore somehow upon them.

How does one wage war against the external world? And how does one release one's visionary soul from the body, and from the constraint of the reason? These may sound like difficult tasks; and yet we all accomplish them every night. In a subjective sense—and Poe's thought is wholly subjective—we destroy the world every time we close our eyes. If *esse est percipi,* as Bishop Berkeley said—if to be is to be perceived—then when we withdraw our attention from the world in somnolence or sleep, the world ceases to be. As our minds move toward sleep, by way of drowsiness and reverie and the gypnagogic state, we escape from consciousness of the world, we escape from awareness of our bodies, and we enter a realm in which reason no longer hampers the play of the imagination: we enter the realm of dream.

—Richard Wilbur, "The House of Poe" (Library of Congress Anniversary Lecture, May 4, 1959), in *The Recognition of Edgar Allan Poe,* ed. Eric. W. Carlson (Ann Arbor: University of Michigan Press, 1966): pp. 256–257, 259.

Douglas Leonard on the Imagery of "The City in the Sea"

[Douglas N. Leonard is the author of articles on Emily Dickinson, Walt Whitman, and other American poets. In this extract, Leonard usefully summarizes the common critical interpretations of the poem, then offers an alternative explanation for its imagery that emphasizes the strangeness and psychological complexity of Poe's imaginative vision.]

Presently there are four fundamental readings of the poem found throughout the body of Poe criticism: (1) the moral one that "the city of sin" (one of Poe's early titles) is being consigned to hell; (2) the cosmic one that the city is all life, all matter, "doomed" (a word from Poe's original title) to re-merge with the primal void; (3) the psychological one that the city is consciousness sinking into subconsciousness (ego into id); and (4) the artistic one (overlapping the psychological) that the city is the product of or represents the imagination, which in order to create must plunge towards its own harrowing destruction. I do not doubt that it was Poe's Romantic intention to allow the poem to vibrate on all these frequencies, appealing to the expectations of as many readers as possible. However, I think that there is a more satisfactory manner in which to construe the imagery of the poem, a way which buttresses a psychological-artistic interpretation. . . .

The movement of [the] light, which originates from below, begins at the town's tallest objects (turrets and pinnacles) and proceeds to its lowest (walls, bowers and shrines). Poe's ordering of these images is not random. Although in the original 1831 version of the poem the eerie light does not move upon the objects in any definite direction at all, in the final version of 1845 the light flows from turrets to shrines and top to bottom in a rather orderly progression. It is understandable that readers have puzzled over this arrangement and endeavored to move the city around in order to make sense of a light source which from "below" illuminates the tallest objects first. Yet the image remains anomalous as long as the city is placed upright, whether under the water or upon the water. There is, however, a third possibility which to my knowledge has never been suggested. The pattern of imagery in the poem makes a great deal more sense if the city is seen as situated under the water upside down, as if hanging by its "base" from the surface of the water. In this way, the ghastly light rising from hell would touch the turrets and pinnacles first and reach the lower walls and shrines last. Further, if the whole city is seen as suspended upside down from the water's surface, the image in the third stanza of the "pendulous" turrets becomes more plausible and the image in the fourth stanza of the city's graves lying level with the waves makes perfect sense.[. . .]

In such a city up and down are inevitably confused by the strain between the unusual perspective and the expectations of everyday reality. Yet, although Poe's vision never comes perfectly clear, the blurring itself is suggestive if the poem represents a vision of the impenetrable imagination which operates on a subconscious level of the mind. Beauty, immutable beauty, resides there, but its strange glory is only partly accessible. [. . .] Apparently, Poe could be of several minds about beauty: it is strange, yet glorious; melancholic, yet blissful; self-destructive, yet immortal. Poe could live with these contradictions even when the result was to obscure both meaning and imagery, as in "The City in the Sea." Obscurity is, of course, to the detriment of Poe the philosopher. One finds a strange obscurity though, for Poe, the poet, apropos.

—Douglas Leonard, "Poe's 'The City in the Sea,'" *The Explicator* 43, no. 1 (Fall 1984): pp. 30–31, 32.

J. LASLEY DAMERON ON POE'S SOURCES FOR "THE CITY IN THE SEA"

[J. Lasley Dameron, Professor of English at Memphis State University, is the co-author of two bibliographical guides to Poe's work, *An Index to Poe's Critical Vocabulary* (1966) and *Edgar Allan Poe: A Bibliography of Criticism, 1827–1967* (1974), as well as the author of many articles on American literature. In this extract, he argues that Poe's poem cannot be traced to a single source, but draws on several, including one that has been overlooked and that provides important insight into the city's bizarre architecture.

Legends and myths of sunken cities and, more recently, the *Revelation* of St. John are cited as the most likely sources for Poe's "The

City in the Sea." Poe's lyric first appeared in 1831 as "The Doomed City," in 1836 as "The City of Sin," and finally, in 1845 under its present title. . . . Critics have recently emphasized that Poe was describing a city "on" the sea rather than "under" it, and have questioned the significance of accounts of sunken cities as sources for the poem. . . .They argue that the imagery of the poem is focused upon a crumbling city positioned upon or just under the surface of the sea. Although Poe's trope of the sinking city may have its primary origin in one or more myths and legends of engulfed or partially engulfed cities—Atlantis, the sunken cities of Sodom and Gomorrah within the Dead Sea, to mention a few—there is little reason to assume that any one source provided the inspiration for the brilliant imagery in Poe's descriptive lyric. One likely, as yet unrecognized, source for some of that imagery is William Scoresby's *Journal of a Voyage to the Northern Whale-Fishery; Including Researches and Discoveries on the Eastern Coast of West Greenland, Made in the Summer of 1822, in the Ship Baffin of Liverpool.* . . . Scoresby's Journal, in line with arguments concerning the influence of the Revelation of St. John. . . , provides additional evidence that the chief sources for Poe's poem are descriptions of cities surrounded by the sea, not engulfed by it.

Scoresby's *Journal* is a scientific account of polar travel, charting four hundred miles of the east coast of Greenland during the summer of 1822. In addition to a variety of carefully documented scientific observations of the arctic landscape and weather conditions, Scoresby records the extraordinary visual effects of natural phenomena associated with the polar regions. One often-described effect is that of atmospheric refraction, which greatly alters the character and appearance of the polar environment and at one point produces illusions of architectural structures that recall those of Poe's poem.[. . .]

Poe's "strange city" where "Death has reared himself a throne" has distinct similarities to the visual distortions of the landscape Scoresby observes along the coastline of eastern Greenland near a region he designates as a whaling area. The cliffs on this coastline are "the color and appearance of real basaltic columns," basalt generally having a gray-to-black color. Through a telescope, the coastline takes on the appearance of unstable, monumental structures, some "suspended in the air," within a filmy or vaporous atmosphere. Scoresby subsequently describes the surface vapor causing such visual refractions as a "transparent stream'" giving "all bodies on the water or near it" a "tremulous motion." Similarly, the "time-eaten towers" of Poe's city in the "dim West" presumably have a dark color which allows "turrets and shadows" to blend, a color also presumably mirrored by the dark, starless sky above and the "melancholy waters" below, at least before the "light from the lurid sea" gives the waves a "redder glow" as the city settled downward. In Poe's city, "all seems pendulous in air;" furthermore, this air is presumably misty because a "void within the *filmy* Heaven" (my italics) will be left by the tops of the slowly sinking towers.[...]

As these parallel passages imply, Scoresby's *Journal of a Voyage to the Northern Whale Fishery* is thus one likely source for some of the vivid imagery that Poe uses in this poem to depict a visionary city, "pendulous" between sky and water in a distant haze of mythic ethereality, that stirs into motion under the eyes of Death (and the reader).

—J. Lasley Dameron, "Another Source for Poe's 'City in the Sea,'" *Poe Studies* 22, no. 2 (December 1989): pp. 43–44.

JOAN DAYAN ON POE AS A TRANSITIONAL FIGURE

[Joan Dayan, Professor of English and African-American studies at the University of Arizona, is the author of *Fables of Mind: An Inquiry into Poe's Fiction* (1987) and *Haiti, History, and the Gods* (1995). In this discussion Poe's poetic "crossbreed" of romance and science, Dayan situates Poe in literary history between Romanticism and Modernism, arguing that his work, especially his long prose-poem *Eureka*, had a significant influence on the Modernist poetic sequence.]

Poe began his writing career as a poet, and throughout his life he questioned the idea of poetry, worried about defining it, and by his own admission, failed to write poems "of much value to the public, or very creditable to myself." And yet, what Poe and his subsequent critics recognize as failure demands further consideration. The problem of Poe's poetry is nothing less than a demonstration of what happens when the lyric of feeling confronts the demands of a form more public and less pure than that celebrated in "The Poetic Principle." The effect of Poe's poetry, whether he willed it or no, is to adulterate "that *Beauty*," which he claimed as "the atmosphere and the real essence of the poem." Poe's alternating longing for and discomfort with the language of romance, and his final attempt to confound his earlier theoretical categories (Truth, Romance, and Poetry) in his scientific, cosmological long poem *Eureka* makes plain the difficult passage from nineteenth-century English poetry to a uniquely modernist poetic.

Eureka, Poe's "Essay on the Material and Spiritual Universe," is his discourse on method and interrogation of poetry. [. . .] As anomalous precursor of "the modern epic," *Eureka* will transform the world of Poetical Science, giving Whitman the right both to declare "there is no more need of romances" (Preface, 1855 *Leaves of Grass*) and to make his coarse, broad composite in honor of "the entire revolution made by science in the poetic method" (Preface, "As A Strong Bird on Pinions Free").[. . .]

Poe's crossbreed, his quest into the parameters of science and poetry, provokes those subsequent sequences founded on the fact of combination. The consistency of "interleaving," whether in a mix of ill-digested remnants (Poe's early poems) or the bold blurring of a poetic idea through prose (*Eureka* and certain tales), opens up the poetic line to generate a new, expansive space of proximate levels, jagged, oblique, and rough. The amorphous, galvanic medium that Poe makes of his prose urges us to rethink the long poem in mechanical terms. What Poe calls "the Cloud-Land of Metaphysics" emerges the locale for poetic language, for Olson's "things on a field," for Williams' "field of action," and finally, for what Valery called "le spectacle idéal de la création du language."

Poe shows how "truth" can be seized by a language that mimes the two tendencies of matter, "attraction and repulsion," convergence and dispersal. And it is no exaggeration to claim that Poe's strategies of reduction and expansion give us a method for discussing the modern poetic sequence: Whitman's *Leaves of Grass*, as well as Pound's *Cantos*, Williams' *Paterson*, and Olson's *Maximus*. The dual insistence on laconic compression and visionary sweep produces that taut unevenness of a journey through Paterson or Dogtown. Perhaps Poe's preface to *Eureka* initiated the dialogue between those poems that refuse closure, that court their own incompleteness, the open road leading from Whitman to his sons, those "Recorders ages hence." These later poetic scenes return us to Eureka in its extraordinary blend of romanticism, science, philosophizing, exhortation, and reverie.

—Joan Dayan, "From Romance to Modernity: Poe and the Work of Poetry," *Studies in Romanticism* 29, no. 3 (Fall 1990): pp. 413–414, 437.

⊛

Elizabeth Phillips on Poe's Early Poems

[Elizabeth Phillips, Professor Emerita of English at Wake Forest University, is the author of many articles on American literature, especially on American women poets and poetry of the sixties. Her critical books include *Edgar Allan Poe: An American Imagination* (1979), *Marianne Moore* (1982), and *Emily Dickinson: Personae and Performance* (1988). In this extract, Phillips argues that the poems Poe wrote before he had notable publishing success are useful in demonstrating the daring and versatility of his poetic gifts.]

The verse from 1825 to 1835 reveals not only the frustrated hopes but also the exceptional gifts of the poet. The fine, sensitive, and often subtle effects that he realized when he was free to explore the pleasures of poetry without trimming his talents for the marketplace are often overlooked. Yet, critic after critic has found early poem after early poem to praise. Although, in most instances, the poem commended by a critic of a particular persuasion is not that chosen by other readers, a gathering of the separate favorable judgments by attentive students of the first poems speaks well for Poe.

The daring, originality, and skill evident in the variety of poetic modes that he tried suggest the value he placed on a *range* of styles. Attention to Poe's ideas has frequently resulted in neglect of his stylistics. When they have been discussed, the tendency is to cite lapses in taste. For example, Robert von Hallberg, after comparing only two brief passages from *Politian* and discussing Poe's criteria for good writing, remarks that his "interest in stylistic range was a fascination for what he must have known he thoroughly lacked as a poet." Poems as different as "I saw thee on thy bridal day" and "The Coliseum," however, belie the claim that he lacks stylistic versatility.

Poe, as W. H. Auden observed, "was interested in too many poetic problems and experiments at once for the time he had to give them." In learning what Auden calls the poet's trade, the young writer took risks. There is, for instance, nothing like the imaginative "Al Aaraaf" in nineteenth-century American literature. But there are also pedestrian poems. There are those to which he returned more than once in an effort—with or without success—to strengthen them. Like Robert Lowell, Poe treated even his printed work as "manuscript" by often revising it for republication. It is in the craft that Poe's tormented perfectionism is perhaps most visible. "To strive for perfection," Halliburton observes, "is to affirm," to say "yes, if not in thunder, at least with a certain insistence."

—Elizabeth Phillips, "The Poems: 1824-1835," *A Companion to Poe Studies*, ed. Eric W. Carlson (Westport, Conn.: Greenwood Press, 1996): p. 87.

Thematic Analysis of
"The Haunted Palace"

"The Haunted Palace" appeared as part of Poe's short story "The Fall of the House of Usher" in 1839. Embedded in this most famous of Poe's tales, the poem bears an important relation to the prose fiction, encapsulating its themes and imagery and contributing to its Gothic gloom, but it also stands as a suggestive lyric in its own right. The poem describes the decline of a "stately palace" from radiance to chaos. Rearing its "head" in "Thought's dominion," the palace is an elaborate conceit for the human mind, the place where consciousness dwells.

As the architecture of the house mirrors the structure of a human head, the palace's fall suggests the disintegration of human consciousness into death and nightmare. At first governed by reason, the head/house is transformed into an anarchy of discordant elements, Poe's symbolic imagery dramatizing a shift from innocence to corruption, sanity to insanity, rational utterance to irrational babbling.

The poem functions as a version of the story within the story. As Dwayne Thorpe observes, the story's narrator is the first "reader" of the poem, interpreting it as a key to Roderick Usher's mental state. The narrator, summoned by his boyhood friend, arrives at the House of Usher (the name of the family as well as the structure they inhabit) and finds it shrouded in "insufferable gloom." Despite his attempts to entertain Roderick and distract him from his melancholy, the narrator can only watch as his mind degenerates with increasing "nervous agitation." The house is dilapidated, and Roderick's mind is likewise "falling apart." The "barely perceptible fissure" that the narrator observes in the wall of the moldering mansion is also the widening rift in Roderick's consciousness. Poe himself wrote that the poem was meant "to imply a mind haunted by phantoms—a disordered brain."

Precipitating this psychic split is the illness and impending death of Roderick's twin sister, Madeline, whose ghostly presence haunts the house. She provides the most recent evidence of an ancestral curse, "a constitutional and a family evil," and Roderick also suffers from a "morbid acuteness of the senses" that is a symptom of this dark legacy. Madeline apparently dies, and the narrator helps Roderick entomb her in the family vault. On a stormy night a week later, however, Roderick's worst suspicions are confirmed and he breaks down in horror, realizing that *"We have put her living in the tomb!"* (Poe's italics). Madeline claws her way out of the sepulchre, appears before them, and falls to her death (this time for real) at Roderick's feet. The narrator flees the house just as it crumbles and is swallowed into the waters of the tarn (a small lake) in which it stands.

Reading the poem in the context of the story aids interpretation of the poem's symbols. Approaching the mansion, the narrator observes "eye-like windows" and believes that the building's weakening construction affects the "morale" of Roderick's existence. In his important essay "The House of Poe," Richard Wilbur describes the way the poem then presents the house as a physical allegory. The "banners yellow, glorious, golden" represent the flowing tresses on a human head. The doorway's "pearl and ruby" suggest the teeth and lips of a mouth. Through this door flows "A troop of Echoes," the faculty of language. As Wilbur explains, the "palace" falls into ruin after the overthrow of the king "Thought": physical corruption symbolizes mental corruption. The clear windows become "encrimsoned windows" (as clear eyes become tortured "bloodshot eyes"), dramatizing a decline from rationality into a hypnagogic state.

Before the "haunting" change takes place, the palace occupies a verdant landscape that suggests a lost world of chivalric romance. In this idyllic place, supernatural forces, "good angels," are in harmony with the natural world. "Gentle air" once "dallied" in this fragrant "happy valley," a fantasy of a lost pastoral. The parenthetical reminder in the second stanza, however, makes clear that "This—all this—was in the olden / Time long ago." This Eden is lost from the outset, creating a mood of nostalgia for a "then" that cannot be recovered in the world of "now." The interior of the palace was also once harmonious and radiant, a place where one could see "spirits moving musically" through the perfect clarity of "two luminous windows." "Porphyrogene," the name of the king, is Poe's own coinage, linked etymologically with "regal," from the purple-draped chamber (the Porphyra) where royal children were born in imperial Constantinople. The "before" scene is characterized by "surpassing beauty" and "wit and wisdom," traits of a well-ordered kingdom and a well-ordered mind.

At the fifth stanza, the crucial adversative "but" interrupts the nostalgic reverie. The palace is "assailed" by evil, sorrow, and mourning.

Poe invites the reader to share in the lament, interposing another parenthetical reminder of the present fallen condition. Desolation is not only inevitable but irrevocable, and the palace's glory "Is but a dim-remembered story / Of the old-time entombed." The final stanza replaces the "wanderers" who joyfully viewed the happy valley with "travelers" who are terrified at its sight. Roderick Usher in effect turns and addresses his companion, a newly arrived traveler, as the word "now" explicitly signals. The phantasmagoric visions that can now be seen in the windows, the "after-the-fall" representations of disturbed mental activity, move to music that is "discordant" and "ghastly." Moreover, the deranged thoughts and maniacal music "rush" from the present into the future with alarming velocity. The dance of the "hideous throng," of language derailed from sense, provokes a sinister laughter that is divorced from pleasure.

This breakdown of language, from sweet music to mad cackling, poses a central tension in the poem. For Poe, language is both a powerful tool of thought and the agent of the destruction of thought. Reading from the "Mad Trist" of "Sir Launcelot Canning" causes events in the romance to cross into the scene of its telling, including the sound of Madeline struggling out of the tomb. Similarly, Roderick's poetic "improvisation" announces his own fate. Poe suggests that the power of these acts of telling, the strange ability of the story-within-the-story and the poem to bring events into being, is ultimately destructive. Moreover, Roderick's poem suggests a masochistic drive inherent in the poet's craft, a deliberate exercising of the potential for the perversion of language, a perversion that destroys the thought that created it. The poem begins with speakers "whose sweet duty / Was but to sing, / In voices of surpassing beauty," but that then speak only "discordant melody." For Poe, who equated poetic utterance with music, the suggestion that language can lead to the very disintegration into lunacy that the poem intends to document creates a troublesome predicament. Roderick Usher is a figure for the poet and he is also, in Thorpe's terms, a "divided hero whose lute produces only wild fantasias."

"The Haunted Palace" dramatizes the ways that language can be both pleasure-giving and destructive. The epigraph to "The Fall of the House of Usher," from the French poet Béranger (1780–1857), emphasizes this sense of the poet/musician as both a powerful creator of music and a passive hearer susceptible to its potentially destructive effects: "Son cœur est un luth suspendu; / Sitôt qu'on le touche il résonne." (His heart is a lute; Touch it, and at once it sounds.) Powerless to control his fate, Roderick Usher pronounces it in song: the "old-time" of harmony, pleasure, and reason has been "entombed," given over to death. As the story suggests, an "interment" can be willful and perhaps premature, leading to disastrous consequences. When thought and language are "time-eaten," they succumb to claustral terror and delirium. ❀

Critical Views on
"The Haunted Palace"

CHARLES BAUDELAIRE ON POE'S PRIMORDIAL PERVERSITY

[French poet and critic Charles Baudelaire (1821–1867) wrote several essays on Poe and translated his work into French. His book of poems, *Les Fleurs du Mal* (1857), is considered a masterpiece and had tremendous influence on Symbolist and Modernist poetry. For Baudelaire, Poe symbolized the poète maudit, the poet as rebel or societal outcast. In this extract, he praises Poe for embracing, as he does in "The Haunted Palace," themes that are central to Baudelaire's own doctrines: faced with "the magnificence of nature shriveling up," the rational yields to the irrational and beauty becomes inseparable from corruption.]

But more important than anything else; we shall see that this author, product of a century infatuated with itself, child of a nation more infatuated with itself than any other, has clearly seen, has imperturbably affirmed the natural wickedness of man. There is in man, he says, a mysterious force which modern philosophy does not wish to take into consideration; nevertheless, without this nameless force, without this primordial bent, a host of human actions will remain unexplained, inexplicable. These actions are attractive only *because* they are bad or dangerous; they possess the fascination of the abyss. This primitive, irresistible force is natural Perversity, which makes man constantly and simultaneously a murderer and a suicide, an assassin and a hangman;—for he adds, with a remarkably satanic subtlety, the impossibility of finding an adequate rational motive for certain wicked and perilous actions could lead us to consider them as the result of the suggestions of the Devil, if experience and history did not teach us that God often draws from them the establishment of order and the punishment of scoundrels;—*after having used the same scoundrels as accomplices!* such is the thought which, I confess, slips into my mind, an implication as inevitable as it is perfidious. But for the present I wish to consider only the great forgotten truth—the primordial perversity of man—and it is not without a certain satisfaction that I see some vestiges of ancient wisdom return to us from a country from which we did not expect them. It is pleasant to know that some fragments of an old truth are exploded in the faces of all these obsequious flatterers of humanity, of all these humbugs and quacks who repeat in every possible tone of voice: "I am born good, and you too, and all of us are born good!" forgetting, no! pretending to forget, like misguided equalitarians, that we are all born marked for evil!

Of what lies could he be a dupe, he who sometimes—sad necessity of his environment—dealt with them so well? What scorn for pseudophilosophy on his good days, on the days when he was, so to speak, inspired! This poet, several of whose compositions seem deliberately made to confirm the alleged omnipotence of man, has sometimes wished to purge himself. The day that he wrote: "All certainty is in dreams," he thrust back his own Americanism into the region of inferior things; at other times, becoming again the true poet, doubtless obeying the ineluctable truth which haunts us like a demon, he uttered the ardent sighs of *the fallen angel who remembers heaven;* he lamented the olden age and the lost Eden; he wept over all the magnificence of nature *shrivelling up before the hot breath of fiery furnaces.*

—Charles Baudelaire, "New Notes on Edgar Poe" (1857). Reprinted in *The Recognition of Edgar Allan Poe*, ed. Eric. W. Carlson (Ann Arbor: University of Michigan Press, 1966): pp. 46–48.

⟨჻⟩

D. H. LAWRENCE ON SLEEP-CONSCIOUSNESS

[Poet, novelist, and critic D. H. Lawrence (1885–1930) is best known for his psychologically complex and sexually frank novels, including *Sons and Lovers* (1913), *Women in Love* (1920), and *Lady Chatterley's Lover* (1928). *Studies in Classic American Literature* (1923), from which this extract is taken, is considered one of the most insightful collections of essays written on American literature. In this passage, Lawrence discusses the transformation that takes place in "The Haunted Palace" as resulting from a problematic mechanical sensitivity to the material world that destroys Usher's "integral soul."]

It is a question how much, once the true centrality of the self is broken, the instrumental consciousness of man can register. When man becomes selfless, wafting instrumental like a harp in an open window, how much can his elemental consciousness express? The blood as it runs has its own sympathies and responses to the material world, quite apart from seeing. And the nerves we know vibrate all the while to unseen presences, unseen forces. So Roderick Usher quivers on the edge of material existence.

It is this mechanical consciousness which gives 'the fervid facility of his impromptus'. It is the same thing that gives Poe his extraordinary facility in versification. The absence of real central or impulsive being in himself leaves him inordinately, mechanically sensitive to sounds and effects, associations of sounds, associations of rhyme, for example—mechanical, facile, having no root in any passion. It is all a secondary, meretricious process. So we get Roderick Usher's poem, *The Haunted Palace,* with its swift yet mechanical subtleties of rhyme and rhythm, its vulgarity of epithet. It is all a sort of dream-process, where the association between parts is mechanical, accidental as far as passional meaning goes.

Usher thought that all vegetable things had sentience. Surely all material things have a *form* of sentience, even the inorganic; surely they all exist in some subtle and complicated tension of vibration which makes them sensitive to external influence and causes them to have an influence on other external objects, irrespective of contact. It is of this vibration or inorganic consciousness that Poe is master: the sleep-consciousness. Thus Roderick Usher was convinced that his whole surroundings, the stones of the house, the fungi, the water in the tarn, the very reflected image of the whole, was woven into a physical oneness with the family, condensed, as it were, into one atmosphere—the special atmosphere in which alone the Ushers could live. And it was this atmosphere which had molded the destinies of his family.

But while ever the soul remains alive, it is the molder and not the molded. It is the souls of living men that subtly impregnate stones, houses, mountains, continents, and give these their subtlest form.

People only become subject to stones after having lost their integral souls.

—D. H. Lawrence, "Edgar Allan Poe" (1923). Reprinted in *Studies in Classic American Literature* (New York: Penguin, 1977): pp. 83–84.

※

T. S. Eliot on Poe's Influence on French Poets

[T. S. Eliot (1888–1965) was one of the most influential poets and critics of the twentieth century. Among his most famous poems are *The Waste Land* (1922) and *Four Quartets* (1944), and among his many volumes of criticism are *The Sacred Wood* (1920), *The Use of Poetry and the Use of Criticism* (1933), and *To Criticize the Critic* (1965), from which this extract is taken. Eliot won the Nobel Prize and the British Order of Merit in 1948. In this essay, Eliot compares Poe's reputation among English and American readers to the figure he presented to the French poets Baudelaire, Mallarmé, and Valéry.]

Before concerning myself with Poe as he appeared in the eyes of these French poets, I think it as well to present my own impression of his status among American and English readers and critics; for, if I am wrong, you may have to criticize what I say of his influence in France with my errors in mind. It does not seem to me unfair to say that Poe has been regarded as a minor, or secondary, follower of the Romantic Movement: a successor to the so-called 'Gothic' novelists in his fiction, and follower of Byron and Shelley in his verse. This however is to place him in the English tradition; and there he certainly does not belong. English readers sometimes account for that in Poe which is outside of any English tradition, by saying that it is American; but this does not seem to me wholly true either, especially when we consider the other American writers of his own and an earlier generation. There is a certain flavor of provinciality about his work, in a sense in which Whitman is not in the least provincial: it is the provinciality of the person who is not at home where he belongs, but cannot get to anywhere else. Poe is a kind of displaced European; he is attracted to

Paris, to Italy and to Spain, to places which he could endow with romantic gloom and grandeur. Although his ambit of movement hardly extended beyond the limits of Richmond and Boston longitudinally, and neither east nor west of these centres, he seems a wanderer with no fixed abode. There can be few authors of such eminence who have drawn so little from their own roots, who have been so isolated from any surroundings. [...]

[I]n Poe, in his life, his isolation and his worldly failure, Baudelaire found the prototype of *le poete maudit*, the poet as the outcast of society—the type which was to realize itself, in different ways, in Verlaine and Rimbaud, the type of which Baudelaire saw himself as a distinguished example. This nineteenth-century archetype, *le poete maudit*, a rebel against society and against middle-class morality (a rebel who descends of course from the continental myth of the figure of Byron) corresponds to a particular social situation. But, in the course of an introduction which is primarily a sketch of the man Poe and his biography, Baudelaire lets fall one remark indicative of an aesthetic that brings us to Valéry:

> "He believed [says Baudelaire], true poet that he was, that the goal of poetry is of the same nature as its principle, and that it should have nothing in view but itself."
>
> 'A poem does not say something—it is something': that doctrine has been held in more recent times.

The interest for Mallarmé is rather in the technique of verse, though Poe's is, as Mallarmé recognizes, a kind of versification which does not lend itself to use in the French language. But when we come to Valéry, it is neither the man nor the poetry, but the *theory* of poetry, that engages his attention. In a very early letter to Mallarmé, written when he was a very young man, introducing himself to the elder poet, he says: 'I prize the theories of Poe, so profound and so insidiously learned; I believe in the omnipotence of rhythm, and especially in the suggestive phrase.' But I base my opinion, not primarily upon this credo of a very young man, but upon Valéry's subsequent theory and practice. In the same way that Valéry's poetry, and his essays on the art of poetry, are two aspects of the same interest of his mind and complement each other, so for Valéry the poetry of Poe is inseparable from Poe's poetic theories.

—T. S. Eliot, "From Poe to Valéry" (1948), in *To Criticize the Critic and Other Writings* (New York: Farrar, Straus and Giroux, 1980): pp. 29, 37. ✍

[John Irwin was Professor and Chairman of the Writing Seminars at the Johns Hopkins University. As John Bricuth, he published the collections of poems *The Heisenberg Variations* (1976). His critical works include *The Mystery to a Solution: Poe, Borges, and the Analytic Detective Story* (1994), *Doubling and Incest/Repetition and Revenge: A Speculative Reading of Faulkner* (1975), and *American Hieroglyphics* (1980), from which this extract is taken. In this chapter, Irwin describes Usher's obsessive fear of death as a struggle with the impossibility of conceiving either an absolute limit (death as the absolute limit of human consciousness) or the absolutely limitless (the infinite abyss). This passage on Poe's analogy of inner and outer space in *Eureka* enables us to appreciate the complexity of thinking that lies behind his spatial analogy in "The Haunted Palace."]

Poe maintains that in using a term like "infinity," anyone

> who has a right to say that he thinks *at all*, feels himself called upon, *not* to entertain a conception, but simply to direct his mental vision toward some given point, in the intellectual firmament, where lies a nebula never to be resolved. . . .The finest quality of Thought is its self-cognizance; and, with some little equivocation, it may be said that no fog of the mind can well be greater than that which, extending to the very boundaries of the mental domain, shuts out even these boundaries themselves from comprehension.

> It will not be understood that, in using the phrase, "Infinity of Space," I make no call upon the reader to entertain the impossible conception of an *absolute* infinity. I refer simply to the "*utmost conceivable expanse*" of space—a shadowy and fluctuating domain, now shrinking, now swelling, in accordance with the vacillating energies of the imagination.

Poe's rhetorical strategy is ingenious. Establishing an analogy between the outer space of physical nature and the inner "space" of temporal consciousness so as to equate the thought of infinity with the infinity of thought, Poe demonstrates that the two spaces are incommensurable. But then on the basis of this analogy (and because the infinite is inconceivable), Poe suggests a substitution of inner space for outer space, of the "boundaries of the mental

41

domain" for the boundless universe. He says that in using "the phrase, 'Infinity of Space'" he does not expect the reader to entertain "the impossible conception of an *absolute* infinity"; rather, he asks him to imagine simply the "'*utmost conceivable expanse*' of space." To the impasse between infinite space and finite mind, between the limitlessness of eternal life and the absolute limit of death, Poe brings a third term—the indefinite; for what he intends to substitute for both the absolutely limitless and the absolutely limited (that is, for the inconceivable) is indeterminacy and the undecidable. The mental domain is not boundless, but what boundaries it has are "shadowy and fluctuating." Indeed, these boundaries may even reverse themselves, since they ultimately depend upon "the vacillating energies of the imagination." The great advantage of the indefinite over the infinite is that, while it may be undecidable, it is not inconceivable. The notion of a shifting or reversible limit, though difficult to imagine, is still not impossible to grasp in an image—the Mobius strip, for example.

—John T. Irwin, *American Hieroglyphics: The Symbol of the Egyptian Hieroglyphics in the American Renaissance* (New Haven: Yale University Press, 1980): pp. 189–190.

⊗

DEBORAH HARTER ON DOUBLING AND FRAGMENTATION

[Deborah A. Harter is the author of *Bodies in Pieces: Fantastic Narrative and the Poetics of the Fragment* (1996). In this essay, Harter describes the unraveling of sanity in "The Haunted Palace" as reflecting the way the doublings in the "House of Usher" create psychic divisions and self-irony.]

[The poem] is the narration of a fragmented, fragmenting voice whose self-irony moves only further and further into a state of perilous division. In Poe's "The Haunted Palace," the subject's "unraveling" is already apparent in the tale that forms its context: "The Fall of the House of Usher" is a dramatic example of fragmentation—of insistent doubling between Roderick and Madeline Usher and the house they inhabit, and of division pulling each one apart. Thus, just as brother and sister have the same floating gray hair, hair of "more than web-like softness," so the house has a gray sedge and minute fungi "hanging in a fine tangled web-work from the evens." As brother and sister wander the house vacantly, eyes perhaps bloodshot with fatigue, so the house has "vacant eye-like windows" that are long, narrow and pointed," and through which "feeble gleams of encrimsoned light" barely glimmer. Just as brother and sister, as twins, both reflect and complete one another, so the house is perfectly duplicated in the muddy tarn that surrounds it, and that reflects "inverted images of the gray sedge, and the ghastly tree stems, and the vacant and eye-like windows". These reflected images, finally, enclosing both house and inhabitants, stare back at a horrified, observing narrator, himself an effect of doubling, an "empirical" other, another part of this multiple consciousness from the moment he is "ushered" into their presence.

But doubling here is also division. Roderick and Madeline, viewed apart from the narrator, seem themselves increasingly the two inadequate halves of a split consciousness, just as the house is fractured in two with its "barely perceptible" zigzag fissure. Their silken hair grows "all-unheeded" just as the house's gray stones are in a "crumbling condition." They are "almost" identical, moreover, sharing "sympathies of a scarcely intelligible nature" but they also "share" parts that can only belong to one or to the other: as though his sister embodied some part of him that has now been lost, as though the two were better as one and cannot be openly viewed in a single glimpse, we see the narrator looking amazedly from Madeline to her brother, only to find this latter with his hands desperately and fully covering his face. With Madeline's apparent decease, Roderick loses any "balance" he might have had and begins, gradually, to acquire his own deathlike features. [. . .]

It is in this degenerating condition, in the very midst of what appears to be a fatal internal struggle, that Roderick writes the poem that is our central concern. He entitles it "The Haunted Palace," and it may be read as the history of the House of Usher, the history of Madeline's devastation, and the history of his own mortal self-battle. It is the story of a consciousness that cannot escape the mechanism of irony that [Paul] de Man describes, but can only become, and this somehow eternally, increasingly divided against itself.

—Deborah Harter, "Divided Selves, Ironic Counterparts: Intertextual Doubling in Baudelaire's 'L'Héautontimorouménos' and Poe's 'The Haunted Palace,'" *Comparative Literature Studies* 26, no. 1 (1989): pp. 28–30. ☙

[Grover Smith was Professor of English at Duke University and is the author of critical studies of Archibald MacLeish, Ford Madox Ford, and T. S. Eliot. In this extract, Smith describes how Poe offered Eliot an archetypal "poet" figure that exerted more influence on him than he may have been willing to acknowledge, especially through the "metaphor of the living death."]

Of the chance of Poe's influence on him, T. S. Eliot professed himself unsure: "one cannot be sure", he said, "that one's own writing has *not* been influenced by Poe." The whole character of Poe's effect on Eliot's poetry, the pressure of a ghost, is bodied forth in this remark. Had any critic but Eliot made it, the title of the essay it comes from could have been "From Poe to Eliot"' instead of "From Poe to Valéry"; for on the score of influencing Symbolist poetry and theory Poe can be claimed for the tradition in which the early Eliot worked largely—and is that not derivatively an "influence"? But by influence Eliot meant something stricter. In "From Poe to Valéry" he appears in harmony with the poetic philosophy and practice of Baudelaire, Mallarmé and Valéry, and with their view of Poe, even while hinting that his own demands for poetry have transcended, without repudiating, theirs. Implicit is Poe's presence in the tradition. But evident is the doubt whether, in Eliot's poetry, Poe ever performed a shaping function, one going beyond his usefulness to poets intermediate in time. I would argue that he did indeed exercise such a function, but with a singular anonymity and unobtrusiveness. [. . .]

Poe gave to Eliot at an early age an archetypal idea of what a poet is. In so far as the young Eliot sensed the significance of Poe as it was to be realised much later, then Poe influenced him. Poe, whatever Eliot's realisation of his value, also oriented him with archetypes of the joylessness and horror in human existence, and these may have penetrated through childhood readings, pre-critically. Poe somehow lent him a primary metaphor, which Eliot would elaborate into a personal myth, the metaphor of the living death. No one who first encountered Poe before reaching the age of 12 (a priceless advantage), as I assume was true of Eliot, could fail to assimilate an extremely deep impression, at a level beneath the formation of theory. By "joylessness and horror" I do not mean anything "spiritual." It is crucial to an understanding of Eliot up to his conversion (1927) that he drew not even from Dante a spiritual mode of poetic feeling. The feeling is always derived from behavior known to the unregenerate; it is experience not under the aspect of eternity but of the world; and he drew from Dante not otherwise than from Poe. Though the first socio-scientific poet, he sought fact not theory, he valued Poe's grotesques for their felt mental abnormalities; and similarly Dante's personages for their suffering, especially their mental suffering: he brought everything down to familiar dimensions of experience. Poe and Eliot are the only modern poets who ring the changes on the agonies of the conscious dead and the entombed living. And in Eliot's poetry certain of Poe's archetypes of horror recur as formal entities again and again.

—Grover Smith, "Eliot and the Ghost of Poe," in *T. S. Eliot: A Voice Descanting*, ed. Shyamal Bagchee (New York: St. Martin's Press, 1990): pp. 149, 150–151.

Thematic Analysis of
"The Raven"

Published in 1845 to tremendous critical and popular acclaim, "The Raven" launched Poe to celebrity status. He took the poem on tour, thrilling audiences with his impassioned reading and brooding looks. In 1846, Poe published "The Philosophy of Composition," a self-promoting essay describing the process by which the poem was written. However exaggerated Poe's step by step account of the genesis of the poem may be, it provides insight into its themes, form, and tone, as well as into Poe's more general theories of poetry. (See extract below.) Today one of the most recognizable poems in American literature, "The Raven" continues to captivate readers with its hypnotizing cadence and melancholy tone.

Each of the poem's 18 stanzas has five octometer lines and a tetrameter refrain, bringing the poem to 108 lines, near to the 100-line measure that Poe conveniently professed to be the ideal length of a poem. The meter is trochaic, giving the poem its characteristic force and gallop. Despite Poe's insistence on his formal ingenuity, the poem closely follows the rhyme scheme of Elizabeth Barrett's "Lady Geraldine's Courtship." Poe greatly admired Barrett's work, dedicating *The Raven and Other Poems* (1845) to her, but he does not acknowledge this debt to her craft.

Poe's "bird of ill omen," as he describes it, joins a company of literary birds from English Romantic poetry, including Coleridge's albatross, Keats's nightingale, and Percy Shelley's skylark. Poe was also likely inspired by Grip, Charles Dickens's raven in *Barnaby Rudge,* a book Poe reviewed in 1841. Critics have pointed out other literary antecedents for Poe's raven, including the biblical account of the ravens feeding Elijah in the wilderness and Hamlet's call, "Come, the croaking raven doth bellow for revenge." Poe's bird is at once a literal and a symbolic presence, a visitor from the dark external world and an emblem of the darkness of grief within the speaker's soul.

The poem begins with the melancholy pondering of a solitary scholar in his chamber, half asleep over "a quaint and curious volume of forgotten lore." Weather sets the mood, a dark winter night that recalls Keats's "In Drear-Nighted December" (1817). The speaker has difficulty ascertaining the source of the sudden "rapping" that startles him out of his morose reverie. From the beginning, the poem addresses a problem of interpretation: the speaker's first response is apprehensive, but he quickly denies the importance of the sound he hears. He searches for clues within the room, his eyes falling on the place where the "dying ember wrought its ghost upon the floor." The image (and the entire scene) recalls Coleridge's "Frost at Midnight" (1798), in which Coleridge refers to the popular superstition that a low blue flame portends the arrival of a visitor. Poe's speaker at first ignores the sign, immersing himself in books to forget the longing he feels for his lost love, Lenore, the visitor who will never again arrive.

The third through sixth stanzas of the poem develop Poe's portrait of the isolated speaker. He has withdrawn from the human community and enclosed himself in a dark room where he experiences "fantastic terrors." The speaker's emotional distress is projected onto his surroundings: the curtains are attributed human feelings with their "sad, uncertain rustling." Giving in to these fanciful imaginings, the speaker is "thrilled" by terror, but he attempts to control his beating heart by "repeating" his hypothesis that the rapping indicates only a visitor's knock. The effort foreshadows the poem's climax: the speaker uses repetition to calm his nerves, but another form of repetition, the nightmarish repetition that the bird introduces, will ultimately escalate, not mollify, his terror. At this point, however, as the speaker insists that he knows what the sound "is," Poe builds suspense—we know that an ordinary explanation will not suffice. Sure enough, the speaker opens the door onto "Darkness there and nothing more." The darkness and silence are undifferentiated, unmarked by any "token" or sign, so the speaker puts forth a word to break that silence—"Lenore?" Oddly, his interrogative comes back as an exclamation. The echo, a repetition that comes from outside himself, heightens his agitation and intensifies his perception of the original tapping sound, which grows "louder." Despite a final effort to investigate the window and deduce a logical explanation, this time attributing the sound to the wind, the speaker's palpitating nervousness increases.

The raven appears. It is a creature out of old mythologies, the "saintly days of yore," and makes an irreverent entrance, awkwardly humanized with an attitude of nobility. It perches "upon a bust of Pallas" (a name for the goddess Athena), an appropriate object for the scholar's room, representing learning and wisdom. The speaker immediately attempts to interpret the bird's presence, to "read into" the ostensibly natural occurrence, and in doing so supplies the "meaning" of what the bird croaks. Poe explains that he chose the word "nevermore" to evoke a melancholy tone in a single non-human utterance. The word has "little meaning—little relevancy" until the speaker interprets its answer as a meaningful answer.

The next eight stanzas present a "dialogue" in which the meaning of the verbal signal "nevermore" is changed as it is repeated. To the speaker's horror, "nevermore" seems to apply to his questions, to make sense. When he tries, reasonably, to reject this notion, by explaining that "what it utters is its only stock and store / Caught from some unhappy master whom unmerciful Disaster / Followed fast and followed faster till his songs one burden bore," he gets caught in the momentum of his own claim. His own words follow faster and faster in a frenzied confusion, and his own "song" begins to imply impending disaster. The observation that the bird "spoke only / That one word, as if his soul in that one word he did outpour," seems to apply to the speaker himself, to his obsessive fixation on the raven's response. Its "melancholy burden" becomes his own.

The raven replies to the student's queries only with relentless negation. It has come to roost on the bust of Pallas, and the despair and grief it brings ultimately overwhelm the goddess's gifts to the intellect. Even though the speaker knows that he supplies the bird's "meaning" by "linking / Fancy unto fancy," he is still deeply disturbed when the bird tells him that he will "nevermore" see his lost Lenore. He is dismayed by the insurmountable fact of her loss. She will nevermore return to his chamber. In his increasing agitation, the raven begins to assume a demonic appearance, its "fiery eyes" burning into his bosom. The chamber's tenebrous atmosphere becomes more lurid and sinister. The raven "replies" that he will nevermore find comfort in any "nepenthe," an ancient grief-banishing drug. As his request for an antidote to suffering is flatly denied, so is his last imploring wish to see Lenore in the afterlife.

As Thorpe has argued, "the narrator is destroyed by his obsessive attachment to an idea powerless to aid but powerful to haunt." The poem reaches its climax in the sixteenth stanza, and the problem of interpretation once again comes to the fore: the speaker does not know whether the raven is prophet or devil, angel or fiend, natural or supernatural. He tries to banish the bird that has haunted him, but cannot rid himself of his tormentor. In desperation and anguish, he commands

"Take thy beak from out my heart, and take thy form from off my door!" He is powerless to escape the negating repetition that the raven offers, and continues to participate in this self-torturing exchange.

The poem ends with a retreat into the world of "shadow." The speaker, entranced by the raven's demonic gaze, sees his soul in the shadow the bird casts on the floor, a soul that "Shall be lifted—nevermore!" With its final "nevermore," the raven refuses to leave, and becomes a permanent reminder of his grief. The poem offers insight into a psychological state that Poe called "that species of despair which delights in self-torture." As Poe explains in "The Philosophy of Composition," the speaker "experiences a phrenzied pleasure in so modeling his questions as to receive from the expected 'Nevermore' the most delicious because the most intolerable of sorrow." Reading the poem in this vein, several critics have interpreted the raven not as a supernatural presence but as a manifestation of the speaker's abnormal psychology, the effect of an internal breakdown. Edward Davidson reads the poem as a case study of a mind that is witnessing its own disintegration. Other critics have argued to the contrary that the poem cannot be explained simply as psychological derangement because the speaker responds to real events, sensory phenomena, and powerful memories. Still others have asked whether Poe was not, in "The Philosophy of Composition" especially, subtly ironizing this kind of psychological interpretation. In any case, problems of judging what is internal or external, mind or environment, form an important tension in the poem.

Whether it is viewed as a story of demonic possession or as a glimpse of the self-effacing effects of grief, "The Raven" has haunted readers since its first publication. The poem was popular with the Pre-Raphaelites, a group of poets and painters in England in the late 1840s, and particularly influenced Dante Gabriel Rossetti's "The Blessed Damozel" (1847), a poem that imagines the scenario of "The Raven" from the point of view of the dead maiden, looking down on her grieving lover from heaven. Various critics have scorned "The Raven" since its first appearance, considering it an "attenuated exercise for elocutionists," but its popularity, as a recitation piece or otherwise, has not waned. Theatrical renditions of this "exercise" still abound in a variety of one-man Poe shows, including a 1997 play starring John Astin, the actor best known for his television role as Gomez Addams. Admired as a sonorous and heartfelt lament and parodied for its squawking "nevermore," Poe's "The Raven" remains unforgettable. ❀

Critical Views on
"The Raven"

EDGAR ALLAN POE ON THE COMPOSITION
OF "THE RAVEN"

[Considered by many to be an example of shameless self-promotion, Poe's famous account of how "The Raven" was written begins by making claims about his predetermined goals for the poem. "The Raven" was ostensibly composed by following Poe's beliefs about the ideal length of a poem (100 lines), the ideal province for poetry (beauty), the ideal tone (sadness), and the ideal structure (use of a brief and sonorous refrain). In the extract that follows, Poe explains that after he conceived of using the raven and decided what it would "say," he determined the topic of his poem.]

I had now gone so far as the conception of a Raven—the bird of ill omen—monotonously repeating the one word, "Nevermore," at the conclusion of each stanza, in a poem of melancholy tone, and in length about one hundred lines. Now, never losing sight of the object *supremeness,* or perfection, at all points, I asked myself—"Of all melancholy topics, what, according to the *universal* understanding of mankind, is the most melancholy?" Death—was the obvious reply. "And when," I said, is this most melancholy of topics most poetical?" From what I have already explained at some length, the answer, here also, is obvious—"When it most closely allies itself to *Beauty:* the death, then, of a beautiful woman is, unquestionably, the most poetical topic in the world—and equally is it beyond doubt that the lips most suited for such topic are those of a bereaved lover."

I had now to combine the two ideas, of a lover lamenting his deceased mistress and a Raven continuously repeating the word "Nevermore"—I had to combine these, bearing in mind my design of varying, at every turn, the *application* of the word repeated; but the only intelligible mode of such combination is that of imagining the Raven employing the word in answer to the queries of the lover. And here it was that I saw at once the opportunity afforded for the effect on which I had been depending—that is to say, the effect of the *variation of application.* I saw that I could make the first query propounded by the lover—the first query to which the Raven should reply "Nevermore"—that I could make this first query a commonplace one—the second less so—the third still less, and so on—until at length the lover, startled from his original *nonchalance* by the melancholy character of the word itself—by its frequent repetition—and by a consideration of the ominous reputation of the fowl that uttered it—is at length excited to superstition, and wildly propounds queries of a far different character—queries whose solution he has passionately at heart—propounds them half in superstition and half in that species of despair which delights in self-torture— propounds them not altogether because he believes in the prophetic or demoniac character of the bird (which, reason assures him, is merely repeating a lesson learned by rote) but because he experiences a phrenzied pleasure in so modeling his questions as to receive from the *expected* "Nevermore" the most delicious because the most intolerable of sorrow. Perceiving the opportunity thus afforded me—or, more strictly, thus forced upon me in the progress of the construction—I first established in mind the climax, or concluding query—that to which "Nevermore" should be in the last place an answer—that in reply to which this word "Nevermore" should involve the utmost conceivable amount of sorrow and despair.

—Edgar Allan Poe, "The Philosophy of Composition" (1846) in *Edgar Allan Poe: Poetry, Tales, & Selected Essays* (New York: Library of America, 1996): pp. 1378–80.

⊗

P. PENDLETON COOKE REVIEWS "THE RAVEN"

[In this 1848 review in the *Southern Literary Messenger,* a magazine to which Poe himself frequently contributed reviews, P. Pendleton Cooke (1816–1850) offers unqualified praise. Cooke lauds Poe's genius, and quotes from Elizabeth Barrett, suggesting the extent of Poe's positive reception abroad.]

"The Raven" is a similarly beautiful poem. Many readers who prefer sunshine to the weird lights with which Mr. Poe fills his sky, may be dull to its beauty, but it is none the less a great triumph of imagination and art. Notwithstanding the extended publication of this remarkable poem, I will quote it almost entire—as the last means of justifying the praise I have bestowed upon it.

The opening stanza rapidly and clearly arranged time, place, etc., for the mysteries that follow.

> Once upon a midnight dreary, while I pondered weak and weary,
> Over many a quaint and curious volume of forgotten lore
> While I nodded, nearly napping, suddenly there came a tapping
> As of some one gently rapping, rapping at my chamber door,
> "'T is some visiter," I muttered, tapping at my chamber door—
>   Only this, and nothing more

Observe how artistically the poet has arranged the circumstances of this opening—how congruous all are. This congruity extends to the phraseology; every word is admirably selected and placed with reference to the whole. Even the word "napping" is well chosen, as bestowing a touch of the fantastic, which is subsequently introduced as an important component of the poem. Stanza 2d increases the distinctness and effect of the picture as already presented to us. The "Midnight Dreary" is a midnight "in the bleak December," and the "dying embers" are assuming strange and fantastic shapes upon the student's hearth. We now pass these externals and some words of exquisite melody let us into the secret of the rooted sorrow which has led to the lonely night-watching and fruitless study. [. . .]

After some stanzas, quaint and highly artistical, the raven is found at the window.[. . .]

The rhythm of this poem is exquisite, its phraseology is in the highest degree musical and apt, the tone of the whole is wonderfully sustained and appropriate to the subject, which, full as it is of a wild and tender melancholy, is admirably well chosen. This is my honest judgment; I am fortified in it by high authority. Mr. Willis says:—"It is the most effective single example of fugitive poetry ever published in this country, and unsurpassed in English poetry for subtle conception, masterly ingenuity of versification, and consistent sustaining of imaginative lift. It is one of those dainties which we *feed on*. It will stick to the memory of every one who reads it.

Miss Barrett says:—"This vivid writing!—this power *which is felt!* 'The Raven' has produced a sensation—a 'fit horror' here in England. Some of my friends are taken by the fear of it, and some by the music. I hear of persons *haunted* by the Nevermore, and one acquaintance of mine, who has the misfortune of possessing a bust of Pallas, never can bear to look at it in the twilight. Our great poet, Mr. Browning, author of Paracelsus, etc., is enthusiastic in his admiration of the rhythm . . . Then there is a tale of his which I do not find in this volume, but which is going the rounds of the newspapers, about mesmerism, throwing us all into most 'admired disorder,' or dreadful doubts as to whether it can be true, as the children say of ghost stories. The certain thing in the tale in question is the power of the writer, and the faculty he has of making horrible improbabilities seem near and familiar."

—P. Pendleton Cooke, "Edgar A. Poe," *Southern Literary Messenger* (January 1848). Reprinted in *The Recognition of Edgar Allan Poe*, ed. Eric W. Carlson (Ann Arbor: University of Michigan Press, 1966): pp. 21–23.

W. H. Auden on Experimentation and Artificiality

[W. H. Auden (1907–1973) was an English-born poet, playwright, and man of letters who settled in the U.S. in 1939 and became a U.S. citizen. He was known for his concern with social realities and leftist politics, and later for his commitment to High-Church Christianity. His poems are gathered in *Collected Shorter Poems 1927–57* (1967) and *Collected Longer Poems* (1969), and his prose in *The Enchafed Flood* (1950) and *The Dyer's Hand* (1962). In this extract, from an essay that was originally the introduction to *Edgar Allan Poe: Selected Prose and Poetry* (1950), Auden addresses some of the problems with "The Raven" and describes how Poe's ingenuity sometimes worked against him.]

His difficulty as a poet was that he was interested in too many poetic problems and experiments at once for the time he had to give to them. To make the result conform to the intention—and the more experimental the intention, the more this is true—a writer has to keep his hand in by continual practice. The prose writer who must earn his living has this advantage, that even the purest hack work is practice in his craft; for the penniless poet there is no corresponding exercise. Without the leisure to write and rewrite he cannot develop to his full stature. When we find fault with Poe's poems we must never forget his own sad preface to them.

> In defence of my own taste, it is incumbent upon me to say that I think nothing in this volume of much value to the public, or very creditable to myself. Events not to be controlled have prevented me from making, at any time, any serious effort in what, under happier circumstances, would have been the field of my choice.

For faulty they must be admitted to be. The trouble with "The Raven," for example, is that the thematic interest and the prosodic interest, both of which are considerable, do not combine and are even often at odds.

In *The Philosophy of Composition* Poe discusses his difficulties in preventing the poem from becoming absurd and artificial. The artificiality of the lover asking the proper series of questions to which the refrain would be appropriate could be solved by making him a self-torturer. The difficulty of the speaker of the refrain, however, remained insoluble until the poet hit on the notion of something nonhuman. But the effect could still be ruined unless the narration of the story, as distinct from the questions and answers, flowed naturally; and the meter Poe chose, with its frequent feminine rhymes, so rare in English, works against this and at times defeats him.

> Not the least obeisance made he;
> not a minute stopped or stayed he;
> But with mien of lord or lady,
> perched above my chamber door.

Here it is the meter alone and nothing in the speaker or the situation which is responsible for the redundant alternatives of "stopped or stayed he" and "lord or lady."

—W. H. Auden, "Edgar Allan Poe" (1950), in *Forewords and Afterwords* (New York: Random House, 1973): pp. 213–214.

[Debra Fried teaches at Cornell University and is the author of several articles on American literature, many of which focus on gender, genre, the use of repetition, and pun. In this extract, Fried describes Poe's use of the refrain in "The Raven" as performing the "work of mourning," examining the poem's relation to the dialogue format, to epitaph, and to the echo song.]

In "The Raven" as in many of Poe's incantatory lyrics, repetition is quite explicitly death, as the work of mourning turns into an act of self-interment by repetition, or "inertia" (to use [Shlomith] Rimmon-Kenan's word) worked by refrain. Repetition kills words, for instance, in a story like Poe's "Berenice," whose narrator is prone "to repeat monotonously some common word, until the sound, by dint of frequent repetition, ceased to convey any idea whatever to the mind." In his fear that monotonous repetition could drain words of meaning, Poe works to free repetition from the killing dangers of monotony. In "The Raven," according to "The Philosophy of Composition," Poe carries out a "design of varying, at every turn, the application of the word repeated," an attempt at variation that allies Poe with Rimmon-Kenan's characterization of good and bad repetition: "Constructive repetition emphasizes difference, destructive repetition emphasizes sameness (i.e., to repeat successfully is not to repeat)." For all Poe's ingenious variations, "The Raven" is a poem about the repetitive work of mourning and of writing, and the price such iterations exact.

In "The Philosophy of Composition" Poe determines that the "only intelligible mode" of varying the application of his refrain from stanza to stanza is "that of imagining the Raven employing the word in answer to the queries of a lover"; that is, the refrain suggests a dialogue format, with the repeated reply varying only insofar as it is a reply to a varying question. In this sense Poe's refrain is like the unvarying retort of epitaphic inscriptions. Like writing, in the terms of Socrates's critique of it in the *Phaedrus*, the raven seems to talk to you as though it were intelligent, but if you ask it anything from a desire to be instructed, it goes on telling you the same thing forever. Its habit of repeating itself reveals that it is as incapable of reasoning, as insentient as an engraved headstone, or a bust of Pallas, or a corpse. Poe's insistence on a dialogue format as the only guarantee of variety within repetition should also remind us of one of the oldest myths of refrain, the voice of Echo, and the scheme of the echo song. "The Raven" figures repetition as unthinking rote transformed by the questioner into repetition as prophecy, threat, or the promptings of the subconscious; similarly, the echo song works its changes by having echo respond as if to a misheard or even mispunctuated version of the questioner's wish, a response that speaks the unacknowledged desire within the question. According to this version of the echo scheme, to speak with echo is to hear the desired answers to our questions and to discover that those answers were implicit in our questions. To call upon echo at all, then, would be in some sense to call upon repetition as a means of revealing to ourselves our deepest desires, desires our words hold but hide. Because when echo answers us "a contrary or self-emending meaning is shown to have been implicit in the original affirmation," echo reveals the power of repetition to "reveal the implicit." In Poe's writings, dialogues, particularly those with a question-and-answer format, are characteristically echoic in the extreme, until replies begin to sound like echoes.

—Debra Fried, "Repetition, Refrain, and Epitaph," *ELH* 53 (1986): pp. 624–625.

B. F. FISHER ON THE FANTASTIC

[Benjamin Franklin Fisher IV is Professor of English at the University of Mississippi and author of many essays on Romantic and Victorian poetry and the Gothic. His works include *The Gothic's Gothic: Study Aids to the Tradition of the Tale of Terror* (1988), and he is the editor of *Poe and Our Times: Influences and Affinities* (1986) and *Poe and His Times: The Artist and His Milieu* (1990). In this extract, Fisher explores the elements of horror fantasy in "The Raven" and considers the interpretation that the poem's speaker engages in a necromantic ritual.]

[The narrator in "The Raven"] concludes his great dramatization of a disintegrating mind, symbolized by the haunting presence of the great black bird—creature of ill omen in many folk beliefs—with this vision [Fisher quotes the final stanza of the poem]. Here is God's—or the devil's—plenty of horror fantasy emanating from the subconscious of the overwrought speaker. The monotony in sound and rhythm effects a hypnotic transition from the mundane to the fantastic. A demonic eye from a frightening bird, an enfeebled sense of wisdom implied in the Pallas connection, and a shadow of death (metaphoric death, which is far more terrifying in this poem than actual physiological demise would be): all are engendered by the powerful visionary imaginings of the student. This speaker's creative imagination bodies forth shapes that remove him more and more from mutuality with others as they destroy his own integration in terms of self.

This man willingly gives in to making analogies between the appearance of the bird, plus its single articulated word, and his own plight. He states this merger categorically:

> Then, upon the velvet sinking, I betook myself to linking
> Fancy unto fancy, thinking what this ominous bird of yore—
> What this grim, ungainly, ghastly, gaunt, and ominous bird of yore
> Meant in croaking "Nevermore."

We might answer this type of querying with the word "nothing," but, as occurs in engaging a Browningesque dramatic monologue, we readers perceive what the speaker may not: that he subjectively imposes negative qualities on the raven, much more so than that the bird is actually a demon or anything other than a natural representative of his species. As the latter, the raven would quite believably be "ungainly," and perhaps "gaunt." But "grim, ghastly, and ominous"? These attributes are imparted from the beholder to the bird instead of vice versa, in all probability. Another possibility exists: that the "quaint and curious volumes of forgotten lore" contain rituals for calling up evil spirits, and that, like a fated character in some tale by M. R. James, say, the narrator unwittingly summons an irrational force that takes shape as a raven. Then, indeed, we could comprehend "the fowl whose fiery eyes now burned into my bosom's core" as something other than a merely imagined horror. We tread a delicate tightrope here. "The Raven" is a poem rife with ambiguities, one of those typical works by Poe, which can yield numerous plausible implications simultaneously—an embarrassment of riches, as it were, to bedevil a reader into a state close to the speaker's as he sits within the raven's shadow at the close.

In other words, we cannot be certain whether to regard the poem as an unfolding of supernatural events, or as a dramatization of the speaker's personal abnormal psychology, or as one more, among many, of Poe's cleverly perpetuated hoaxes. Any alternative is possible, and these three are by no means exhaustive. The music in this poem can "enchant" readers as well as the speaker, and Poe gives us no absolute meaning.

—B. F. Fisher, "Fantasy Figures in Poe's Poems," in *The Poetic Fantastic: Studies in an Evolving Genre,* ed. Patrick D. Murphy and Vernon Hyles (New York: Greenwood Press, 1989): pp. 45–46.

⚈

LELAND PERSON ON THE SELF-DECONSTRUCTION OF "THE RAVEN"

[Leland Person Jr. teaches at Southern Illinois University and is the author of *Aesthetic Headaches: Women and a Masculine Poetics in Poe, Melville, and Hawthorne* (1988) and several articles on Hawthorne, Henry James, Fenimore Cooper, and other American writers. In this essay, Person considers Poe's self-reflexive process of reading and writing "The Raven," showing how "The Philosophy of Composition" self-deconstructs to become "another version of the work it purports to critique." As the student in the poem is reading the raven, Poe and the reader are reading "The Raven."]

As early as 1850 George Washington Peck suggested that in "The Philosophy of Composition" Poe "carried his analysis to such an absurd minuteness, that it is a little surprising that there should be any [one] verdant enough not to perceive that he was 'chaffing.'" Peck even compared the essay to Poe's "harmless hoaxes," at the end of which the author "cries 'sold!' in our faces." Much like "The Purloined Letter," which Poe published just prior to "The Raven," and which has been exhaustively analyzed for its intricate doublings of texts and authors, I think "The Philosophy of Composition" can be regarded, although in a different sense than Daniel Hoffman has suggested, as a "put-on": ostensibly a critical essay that becomes another version of the work it purports to critique. By conflating the processes of reading and writing so that reading becomes rewriting, Poe subverts the very sort of scientific or mathematical certainty that he seems to be praising and illustrating in his essay. Put another way, he deconstructs not only his own "philosophy of composition," but philosophy itself—making philosophy essentially synonymous with composition. Furthermore, the deconstruction to which Poe subjects "The Raven" in "The Philosophy of Composition" can also be observed in the poem itself. Reading the raven, no less than reading "The Raven," means writing, or composing, a philosophy. [. . .]

As readers, for example, our relationship to "The Raven" parallels the student's relationship to the raven, which figures in the poem as a kind of primitive "speaking" text. At the most basic level, both the reader outside the text and the student inside it are trying to read "The Raven." The raven, like the poem with which it is synonymous, utters a word whose meaning must be interpreted, although this is not to say that the raven is the author of the word "Nevermore." The bird is really identical with the word it speaks, since it possesses no intentionality and no other words. Poe himself, in fact, explicitly links the student with the reader, maintaining that the "revolution of thought, or fancy, on the lover's part [near the end of the poem], is intended to induce a similar one on the part of the reader—to bring the mind into a proper frame for the *denouement*—which is now brought about as rapidly and as *directly* as possible." David Halliburton calls the relationship between the bird and the student a "reciprocity," but the relationship is not truly reciprocal, since the student controls the meaning of the bird's utterance—what Poe calls the "effect of the *variation of application.*"

Furthermore, in the poem as in the essay Poe demonstrates that the student's attempt to "read" and understand the raven's word (or "philosophy") involves him necessarily in an effort to rewrite, or "compose," the raven. While the raven ("The Raven") utters only a word—only itself—the student (the reader) manipulates the text in order to make it mean what he wants it to mean.[. . .]

Not simply the effect of the raven's utterance, but its meaning derives from the subjective process of "linking fancy unto fancy." Michael Williams has observed that "in 'The Raven,' as in Poe's works generally, [the ideal sign] is revealed as a function of interpretive desire." The same thing can be said about "The Philosophy of Composition," for in the process of reading and rewriting the poem in that essay, Poe makes it clear that the intention, or effect, of both reading and writing is an "air of consequence." Poe notes at one point in the essay that the "next *desideratum* was a pretext for the continuous use of the one word 'nevermore,'" but in fact the only "pretext," at least for the raven's speech, is the poem or composition—actually a series of compositions—in which the word is inscribed. Pretext and text become the same.

—Leland S. Person, Jr., "Poe's Composition of Philosophy: Reading and Writing 'The Raven,'" *Arizona Quarterly* 46, no. 3 (Autumn 1990): pp. 1-2, 8, 12.

(꩜)

Dave Smith on Poe as a Southern Writer

[A poet, critic, and Professor of English at Louisiana State University, Dave Smith is the author of several books of poetry, including *Homage to Edgar Allan Poe* (1981), *The Roundhouse Voices* (1985), and *Floating on Solitude* (1996). His critical works include *Local Essays: On Contemporary American Poetry* (1985), and a collection of essays on the poet James Wright. He is the editor of *The Essential Poe* (1991). In this essay, Smith summarizes Poe's perhaps parodic use of the set pieces of melodrama, and then considers "The Raven" in the context of a regional experience of loss, despite its lack of local detail.]

"The Raven," unequivocally the most famous of Poe's small body of poetry, may be among our most famous *bad* poems. Americans are fond of saying we do not read and do not care for poetry. It may be so. Yet Americans commonly recognize Poe's bird as subject of a poem by a weird guy who drank himself to death. Written and published in 1845, in print steadily for 148 years, the stanzas of "The Raven" are sonic flashcards. We may not know Whitman, Dickinson, Frost, or Eliot. But we do know Poe. We know "The Raven."

A poem that might have been designed by Benjamin Franklin, "The Raven" purports to be explained by Poe's "Philosophy of Composition." Poe wrote his essay for crowds smitten by his bird. Interestingly, he does not justify poetry with morality, as Emerson and Whitman would. He pretends to expose the poet's trade. Some recent criticism has seen "The Raven" as a parody of Romantic poems of personal discovery. Perhaps. What Poe leaves unsaid peels, layer by layer, toward two questions answerable only by speculation. The first asks why "The Raven" has for fifteen generations commanded the imaginations of people who have often enough known it to be a bad poem. The second question asks if Poe is a Southern writer. They are related questions.

That "The Raven" is a bad poem is unacceptable to many readers, and Poe people are not swayed much by rational argument. Were they, the plot alone would convict Poe. A man sits late in a storm; he laments a lost lady love; a bird not ordinarily abroad at night, and especially not in severe weather, seeks entrance to the human dwelling; admitted, the bird betrays no fright, no panic, its attitude entirely focused on its host—an invited guest; the bird, then, enters into a ventriloquial dialectic with the host and is domesticated to become an inner voice; we might say it is the voice of the *inner ground* as opposed to *underground,* which word means much to the American spirit with its reasons to run, to hide, to contain itself. Action then ceases.

Poe knew this one-man backlot production for the smoker it was. His embrace of gothic machinery includes a terrified, obsessed man, an inhospitable, allegorical midnight in December, a "gifted" animal, extreme emotional states, heavy breathing of both cadence and melodramatic signifiers (*grim, gaunt*), the supernatural presence of inexplicables (perfume, Pallas, bird), all to portray a psychic battle in the mind. Poe assembles a version of saloon theater for the mind's ear. [...]

If we read "The Raven," despite its absence of specific local details, as an "awareness" of the life of America in 1845, we see that Poe has conjectured the nightmare of the individual cut off from history, abandoned by family, place, and community love. He experiences personally what the South will experience regionally and the country will, down the long road, experience emotionally. Though he means to celebrate Lenore, what he most intensely celebrates is the union with community, the identity of place and people which Poe simultaneously has and has lost. In this, in 1845, he speaks for the Southern white and, paradoxically, for the slave paralyzed in his garden and also dispossessed. This story is still the nightmare. Having seen it, Poe celebrates the sensibility or imagination that suffers and knows simultaneously, ultimately the figure of the artist. This figure will sit in the lost garden, knowing its lostness, without explanation, but aware that the change is hopeless and continuous. This poem will, in its late variations, become our outlaw song of the renegade, the cowboy in black, the rebel without a cause. "The Raven" is the drama of nightmare awakening in the American poetic consciousness where there is no history which is not dispossession, little reality to the American promise, and nothing of consequence to place trust in except the song, the ode of celebration.

—Dave Smith, "Edgar Allan Poe and the Nightmare Ode," *Southern Humanities Review* 29, no. 1 (Winter 1995): pp. 4-5, 9-10.

Thematic Analysis of
"The Bells"

For readers who first think of Poe as the fiction writer who inaugurated the rational inquiries of the detective story, a poem like "The Bells" seems out of character, a withdrawal from thought and logic into sensation and even nonsensical fantasy. As Alan Shucard points out, this "other Poe" aims poems at the body, not the mind, giving pleasure through the ears, not the intellect. In light of other poems in his oeuvre, however, "The Bells" marks only the extreme of Poe's career-long experiments with the acoustic effects of language. An extended exercise in onomatopoeia, the poem has become a textbook example of the use (or overuse) of words that sound like their referents, such as "shriek" and "groan." Jeffrey Meyers calls the poem a "somewhat mechanical, onomatopoeic, forced *tour de force.*"

The poem offers an important example of Poe's musical theories of poetry in practice. In "The Rationale of Verse," a lengthy technical essay about English prosody published in the *Southern Literary Messenger* in 1848, Poe puts forth the idea that pleasure in poetry originates from a quantitative apprehension of "equality" in auditory symmetries. (See extract below.) The reader of "The Bells" is immediately aware of the repetition of words and the symmetries of rhyme. In "The Poetic Principle," Poe offers his famous definition of poetry as the "rhythmical creation of beauty" and "The Bells" certainly exploits rhythmic effects. (See extract after Critical Views on "The City in the Sea.") But Poe's poetic principle also requires "a wild effort to reach the Beauty above." Through the music of poetry, he explains, "we attain to but brief and indeterminate glimpses" of divine and rapturous joys." "The Bells" may not live up to these lofty ideals, but it does demonstrate the masterful manipulation of words to suggest their values beyond their usual semantic meanings.

The composition of "The Bells" allegedly began in May 1847 at the suggestion of Marie Louise Shew, the nurse who cared for Poe and his wife during their illnesses, and to whom Poe later developed a romantic attachment. Suffering from writer's block, Poe complained that ringing bells in the street were disturbing him, and Shew apparently urged him to write a poem about them, starting lines for him to finish. The poem was published posthumously late in 1849.

The poem begins with forward-looking joy and ends with backward-looking sorrow. Each of the four stanzas describes a different kind of bell, each one representing a different life phase and the emotional states that correspond to it—courtship, marriage, crisis, and mourning (Thorpe, see extract below). The first stanza presents sledge (sleigh) bells in a scene of "merriment" and "melody." Brisk *i* sounds help create the feeling of an "icy air of night," and the *-inkle* rhymes convey high-pitched excitement. In line 11, "tintinnabulation" is Poe's own coinage for the ringing of bells. (*The Oxford English Dictionary* lists the word as first used in this poem in 1831.) Poe takes the liberty of making up a word, in keeping with his emphasis on originality in poetry and his belief in the elasticity of language as a musical medium. In the last lines of each stanza, Poe further manipulates the medium of words for its musical potential. Once the trochaic rhythm is strongly established, it carries through the sevenfold repetition of the word "bells" as if the words varied alternately in weight. Designing the poem to be read aloud, Poe plays with the "palpable" quality of the word "bells" to create variability in repetition.

In the second stanza, wedding bells are evoked with resonant long-o sounds. The change in vowels mimics the change in the bells' tone: these bells announce a world of "happiness" and "harmony" that builds on the "melody" of courtship. As the sledge bells do, the wedding bells optimistically "foretell" future delight, but they have a richer, more sensuous sound coming through the "balmy air of night." The sonorousness phrase "molten-golden notes" creates the "gush of euphony" that Poe then describes. With sweetness that is too cloying, perhaps, the wedding bells foretell a "swell" of fecundity and happiness in a mood of liquid ease, and the images of "turtle-dove" and "moon" invite associations with love and fertility. A still-longer chain of "bells" concludes this stanza. With heightened awareness of words as sounds, the reader imagines hearing the bells in the poem's own "rhyming and chiming."

The third stanza jars the reader with its sudden and strident evocation of alarm bells. Their bold clanging introduces discord without warning, a "tale of terror" and "turbulency." Poe intensifies the sense of startling disruption by employing long-e sounds: alarm bells sound in the night and provoke the "shriek" and "scream" of those "too horrified to speak." ("Eek" is, after all, the onomatopoeic rendering of a human exclamation for fright.) Poe is in his element in this stanza, spinning off lines about "clamorous appealing," "mad expostulation," and "desperate desire." He lapses into melodrama, lavishing on lines about the "clang and clash and roar" and the "horror they outpour / In the bosom of the palpitating air!" All the "twanging," "clanging," and "jangling" are enough to give the reader a headache. The discordant sounds of the words imitate the discord they describe. In the last lines of the stanza, Poe presents a skillful internal rhyme, linking "anger" and "clangor" to draw together the impassioned human response to disaster and the sensory nightmare.

Poe turns down the volume in the fourth stanza with the description of iron funeral bells. In this post-disaster scene, the long-o sounds, especially the -one rhymes, convey not mellowness but lugubriousness. In this "world of solemn thought," the bells toll a "monody," an elegy or ode of lament. The "meaning of the tone" is, sadly, well known to the listeners. The unnamed tragedy that caused such alarm is now in the past, but its effects continue to be felt. The bells are now a reminder, not a portent of the future. In a strange tangential expansion, Poe suggests that the mourning dehumanizes the mourners: "They are Ghouls." While this shift may be seen as Poe reaching into his usual bag of ghoulish tricks, he does add a new dimension to the poem—the song of mourning is bizarrely transformed into a "pæan," a song of joyous exultation, by the king of the ghouls. The sleigh ride's "Runic rhyme" reappears, this time with macabre cheer in an ancient pagan frenzy. But this wild sound degenerates again into "sobbing." The bells "knell" and "toll" once more. Each stanza of "The Bells" is longer than the one before it, and this fourth and longest stanza, contorted through a ghoulish fantasy, suggests the protraction of suffering that grief brings.

Linking "tone," "groan," and "alone," "throats" and "floats," and other words throughout the poem, Poe creates the "muffled monotone" he describes. The poem is at once a description and a performance of the moods he presents, a catalog of sound effects and a source of sound effects. Understandably, the poem has been criticized as shallow, as a show-offish display of songster skills. The poem is still used as a recitation piece for children, but can be appreciated as more than simply clever. Poe thoroughly exploits the musical potentialities of words, testing the limits of their resounding power. ❈

Critical Views on
"The Bells"

[In this essay, published in the *Southern Literary Messenger* in 1848, Poe expands on material from "Notes upon English Verse," a shorter essay published in *The Pioneer*, March 1843. As a technical study of prosody, it has been criticized as puzzling and even in error, but the essay presents Poe's theorizing about the importance of symmetry and repetition, later developed in *Eureka*. Arguing that the primitive basis of poetry is spondaic, a metrics of simple equality, Poe goes on to describe the increasing complexity of verse in a fallen world. He identifies "the perception of pleasure in the equality of *sounds*" as the primary principle of music, and applies this principle to poetry.]

Verse originates in the human enjoyment of equality, fitness. To this enjoyment, also, all the moods of verse—rhythm, metre, stanza, rhyme, alliteration, the *refrain,* and other analogous effects—are to be referred. As there are some readers who habitually confound rhythm and metre, it may be as well here to say that the former concerns the *character* of feet (that is, the arrangements of syllables) while the latter has to do with the *number* of these feet. Thus by "a dactylic *rhythm*" we express a sequence of dactyls. By "a dactylic hexa*meter*" we imply a line or measure consisting of six of these dactyls.

To return to *equality.* Its idea embraces those of similarity, proportion, identity, repetition, and adaptation or fitness. It might not be very difficult to go even behind the idea of equality, and show both how and why it is that the human nature takes pleasure in it, but such an investigation would, for any purpose now in view, be superrogatory. It is sufficient that the *fact* is undeniable—the fact that man derives enjoyment from his perception of equality. Let us examine a crystal. We are at once interested by the equality between the sides and between the angles of one of its faces: the equality of the sides pleases us; that of the angles doubles the pleasure. On bringing to view a second face in all respects similar to the first, this pleasure seems to be squared; on bringing to view a third it appears to be cubed, and so on. I have no doubt, indeed, that the delight experienced, if measurable, would be found to have exact mathematical relations such as I suggest; that is to say, as far as a certain point, beyond which there would be a decrease in similar relations.

The perception of pleasure in the equality of *sounds* is the principle of *Music*. Unpractised ears can appreciate only simple equalities, such as are found in ballad airs. While comparing one simple sound with another they are too much occupied to be capable of comparing the equality subsisting between these two simple sounds, taken conjointly, and two other similar simple sounds taken conjointly. Practised ears, on the other hand, appreciate both equalities at the same instant—although it is absurd to suppose that both are *heard* at the same instant. One is heard and appreciated from itself: the other is heard by the memory; and the instant glides into and is confounded with the secondary appreciation. Highly cultivated musical taste in this manner enjoys not only these double equalities, all appreciated at once, but takes pleasurable cognizance, through memory, of equalities the members of which occur at intervals so great that the uncultivated taste loses them altogether.

—Edgar Allan Poe, "The Rationale of Verse" (1848). Reprinted in *Edgar Allan Poe: Poetry, Tales, & Selected Essays* (New York: Library of America, 1996): pp. 1393–1394.

⊛

WILLIAM CARLOS WILLIAMS ON POE'S WORDPLAY

[A physician and poet, William Carlos Williams (1883–1963) was an important innovator in Modernist poetry whose poems distilled observed moments and presented them with objective lucidity. His books include *Spring and All* (1923), *Paterson* (1946–1958), *Pictures from Breughel*, which won a Pulitzer Prize in 1964, and *In the American Grain* (1925), a collection of critical essays from which this extract is taken. Williams admires Poe's "reawakened genius of place" and aims to redeem Poe's reputation from some of the critical charges against him: "Poe was

NOT, it must be repeated, a Macabre genius, essentially lost upon the grotesque and arabesque. If we have appraised him a morass of 'lolling lilies,' *that* is surface only." In this extract, Williams describes Poe's effort to dissociate words from their ordinary usages, an attempt that Williams attributes to Poe's "sense of a beginning" rooted in local soil.]

With Poe, words were not hung by usage with associations, the pleasing wraiths of former masteries, this is the sentimental trap door to beginnings. With Poe words were figures; an old language truly, but one from which he carried over only the most elemental qualities to his new purpose; which was, to find a way to tell his soul. Sometimes he used words so playfully his sentences seem to fly away from sense, the destructive! with the conserving abandon, foreshadowed, of a Gertrude Stein. The particles of language must be clear as sand. [...]

This was an impossible conception for the gluey imagination of his day. Constantly he labored to detach SOMETHING from the inchoate mass—That's it:

His concern, the apex of his immaculate attack, was to detach a "method" from the smear of common usage—it is the work of nine tenths of his criticism. He struck to lay low the "*niaiseries*" [foolishnesses] of form and content with which his world abounded. It was a machine-gun fire; even in the slaughter of banality he rises to a merciless distinction. . . . He sought by stress upon construction to hold the loose-strung mass off even at the cost of an icy coldness of appearance; it was the first need of his time, an escape from the formless mass he hated. It is the very sense of a beginning, as *it is the impulse which drove him to the character of all his tales*; to get from sentiment to form, a backstroke from the swarming "population."

He has a habit, borrowed perhaps from algebra, of balancing his sentences in the middle, or of reversing them in the later clauses, a sense of play, as with objects, or numerals which he *has* in the original, disassociated, that is, from other literary habit; separate words which he feels and turns about as if he fitted them to his design with *some* sense of their individual quality: "those who belong properly to books, and to whom books, perhaps, do not quite so properly belong."

The strong sense of a beginning in Poe is in *no one* else before him. What he says, being thoroughly local in origin, has some chance of being universal in application, a thing they never dared conceive. Made to fit a *place* it will have that actual quality of *things* anti-metaphysical——

About Poe there is—
No supernatural mystery—
No extraordinary eccentricity of fate——

He is American, understandable by a simple exercise of reason; a light in the morass—which *must* appear eerie, even to himself, by force of terrific contrast, an isolation that would naturally lead to drunkenness and death, logically and simply—by despair, as the very final evidence of a too fine seriousness and devotion.

—W. C. Williams, *In the American Grain* (Norfolk, Conn.: New Directions, 1925): pp. 221–222.

❦

DANIEL HOFFMAN ON POE AS CRAFTSMAN

[Daniel Hoffman was Professor of English and Poet in Residence at the University of Pennsylvania and taught at several other universities. His books include many volumes of poetry and criticism, including *Form and Fable in American Fiction* (1961), *Barbarous Knowledge: Myth in the Poetry of Yeats, Graves, and Muir* (1967), and works on William Faulkner, Stephen Crane, and Carl Sandburg. In this extract, Hoffman explores Poe's emphasis on thought and conscious craft as essential to poetic composition. Hoffman suggests that Poe's insistence on technical control liberates, not stifles, poetic energies, inducing a state in which "the mind is so completely occupied with the management of verse technique that it cannot interfere with that subliminal allegory flowing beneath the manifest level of mental activity."]

Yes, the Mind in control of the passions which afflict the Heart becomes the guiding pilot conducting Poe's tripartite Self upward to the realms and regions properly the Soul's. Therefore Poe's concentration upon himself as craftsman is not mere vanity, or an aberrant infatuation with his own verbal resources. No, he must attend to the use of the power tools which shape his poetry, for it's the power as much as the craft that he wants to be sure of wielding. The intellectual power. Even if to wield it he must pretend (or maybe even actually convince himself) that the poem, the work of art, is a wholly conscious construct. That way, the poet is completely in charge of the manipulation of his own sufferings.

It would appear that one set of needs is served by Poe's insistence upon the obligatorily ratiocinative method of his composition, another by his obligatory subject and tone. What is the relation between his claim that imagination is a rational and orderly premeditated process and his need to drape it in crepe at the bier of a beautiful woman? What is the connection but that the straitjacket method enables the poet to deal with his obsessive and inescapable subject by compelling him to think about something else, something other than the woe vibrating within him which to think of would overcome him. So the method of his art enables the madness of his matter to be spoken.

But surely this cannot account for the influence of Poe's philosophy on the symbolist poets? Oh, but it can. Just as Poe (or Yeats, or Swinburne) would put the intellect to sleep with the regularity and insistence of their cadences, so as to liberate the free association of the matter of the unconscious, so too can those associative processes be encouraged when the mind is so completely occupied with the management of verse technique that it cannot interfere with that subliminal allegory flowing beneath the manifest level of mental activity. That is why, in a good poem, form is the tensor of theme.

—Daniel Hoffman, *Poe Poe Poe Poe Poe Poe Poe* (New York: Vintage Books, 1985): pp. 92–93.

[Dwayne Thorpe teaches at Washington and Jefferson College and is the author of several articles on Poe's poetry and poetic theory. In this passage, Thorpe explains that critical disapproval of Poe's poetry in part reflects a trend toward de-emphasizing the musical elements of verse, a trend counter to Poe's "insistent musicality." Thorpe then offers a reading of "The Bells" that shows how Poe's evocative music is expressive.]

This contrast between Poe's passion for his poems and the critics' indifference to them is the essential fact confronting anyone who studies them, and it needs to be understood. Critics have neglected Poe's poetry partly because he wrote so little of it; partly because his best fiction is very good, indeed; partly because the poetry has primarily influenced non-English poets; but chiefly because it runs against the stream. This is most obvious in his insistent musicality. Poe defined poetry as "the rhythmical creation of beauty" even as Emerson was laying down a new law that "it is not metres, but a metre-making argument that makes a poem"; and twentieth-century American poets have built on the image, not the musical phrase.[. . .]

Suggestiveness is the hallmark of Poe's verse. Since poetry is about what cannot be named, its essence lies in evocative music, and his poetry is a gallery of strategies of suggestion, each one new. "The Bells," for instance, is a tour de force that expresses meaning entirely through musicality. The author of a popular book on public speaking had suggested to Poe that a poem for recitation, offering great variety of vocal expression, could achieve both fame and profit, and Poe responded with this virtuoso exploration of onomatopoeia. But "The Bells" is considerably more than sound effects. Inattentive readers hear in it only the sounds of four different kinds of bells, and even expert readers (Auden; Stovall 1969) sometimes miss the point. As the poem moves from silver to gold to brass to iron, its tonal shifts evoke attendant emotions, settings, and activities, and finally the shape of a life divided into four stages: courtship, marriage, crisis, and mourning. Meaning wells up from music, the bells that mark the stages of life. This can be seen in the evolution of a single line through the poem's four stanzas.

What a world of merriment their melody foretells!

· · · · ·

What a world of happiness their harmony foretells!

· · · · ·

What a tale of terror, now, their turbulency tells!

· · · · ·

What a world of solemn thought their monody compels!

The slide from merriment to solemnity accompanies a shift from future to present, the fatal "now," and ends with a new verb marking the power of time to force the mind. "Melody" and "harmony," the music before the fall, dissolve here as in "The Haunted Palace."

The metamorphosis of this line reveals the pattern of the poem: a pattern noted by readers who attend to the music's variations. As time overshadows the carefree life of the opening, so it dominates the poem's expanding stanzas. The first stanza has fourteen lines, the second twenty-one, the third thirty-four, and the last forty-four. The first two stanzas, describing the happiness of life before knowledge of loss, have less than half the length of the last two. Thus, structure weights the poem toward darkness.

—Dwayne Thorpe, "The Poems: 1836–1849." Reprinted in *A Companion to Poe Studies,* ed. Eric W. Carlson (Westport, Conn.: Greenwood Press, 1996): pp. 90, 94–95.

Thematic Analysis of
"Annabel Lee"

Many critics have considered "Annabel Lee," Poe's last poem, to be his elegy for his wife Virginia, who died of tuberculosis in January 1847, more than two years before the poem's composition in May 1849. Read in light of biographical circumstances, the poem suggests the psychological effects of this event, but it is important to remember that the poem also reflects Poe's stated aesthetic belief that "the death . . . of a beautiful woman is, unquestionably, the most poetical topic in the world." The mourning of the death of a young maiden was a favorite topic that he had been utilizing since his earliest poetry. After Poe's death, several women claimed that they had inspired the poem, but it likely reflects a composite sketch that Poe transformed into this idealized portrait.

Arguably, the poem, as well as Poe's career-long thematic preference, is a response to the deaths of "beautiful women" that considerably predate Virginia's. Meyers forcefully summarizes the major themes of Poe's work as they reflect these losses. Poe is preoccupied with

> victimization, power and powerlessness, confrontations with mysterious presences, extreme states of being, dehumanization and its cure, the relation of body and soul, memory of and mourning for the dead, the need for spiritual transcendence and affirmation. Poe's beliefs that the dead are not entirely dead to consciousness, his hope that love could transcend death, and his apprehension of beauty beyond the grave were inspired by the early deaths of his mother, of Jane Stanard (the idealized mother of a school friend), and of Frances Allan (his foster mother).

These themes culminate in "Annabel Lee." By introducing his subject as a maiden "whom you may know," he presents a universalized dead woman and a fictional dead woman for the purposes of the poem, all with a conversational ease that suggests an intimate subject and an intimate audience. Because the poem conveys this familiarity, perhaps, almost as if the speaker were disclosing his sorrow to the reader alone, this poem has invited more autobiographical interpretations than Poe's other versions of the lament for a beautiful woman.

Before his unexpected death, Poe ensured the poem's publication by giving it to his literary executor, Rufus Griswold, to the editor John Thompson in payment for a debt, and also to *Sartain's Union Magazine*. Griswold included it in his obituary, and it appeared the next month in Thompson's *Southern Literary Messenger*, but not until the following year in the magazine to which Poe had originally sold it. As he had with most of his poems, Poe capitalized on whatever angles for publication he could.

By choosing to write a ballad, Poe drew on the folk traditions of story-songs and gave his poem an archaic feel. He uses the traditional English ballad form, alternating tetrameter and trimeter lines, and employs an anapestic rhythm that makes the poem, to many modern readers, sound inadvertently comic. He also uses a great deal of repetition and parallelism, a characteristic of ballads that Coleridge, whose criticism Poe greatly admired, considered an integral part of the ballad's approach to emotionally charged material— a ballad repeated statements too strong to be said only once. Longing for a time "long ago," Poe sets his story in an old-fashioned "kingdom" reminiscent of fairytales, a romantic backdrop against which his tale appears timeless.

Poe begins the poem by describing a perfect mutual love, a love that was exclusive of all "thought" other than the consideration of its reciprocity. Stressing that "*She* was a child and *I* was a child," Poe equalizes their contributions to the love affair, a line that has raised the eyebrows of those who consider the poem to be about his marriage to his child cousin. Without oversimplifying the poem by claiming that Poe is addressing criticism of the age difference between himself and his deceased wife, we can read the line as insisting on child-like innocence in both parties. This sense of purity and ideality, now irrecoverably lost, is redoubled in the poem's most poignant line: "But we loved with a love that was more than love." Using repetition to suggest the circularity and insufficiency of the attempt to describe this ideal passion, Poe posits a love so pure that the word "love" cannot encompass it.

This consideration of a love beyond human love invites supernatural elements. Poe explains that even the angels were jealous of this love, and that spiteful seraphic vigilance compelled them to inflict suffering on the lovers. Poe states that "this was the reason" for Annabel Lee's death, a logic of celestial cause that finds vengeance behind the "chilling wind" that precipitated her death. At the same time, Poe curiously blends the natural and supernatural, as "chilling and killing" also suggests the all-too-real circumstances of death from tuberculosis. Worldly concerns assert themselves in the poem, even among references to heavenly influences. Annabel Lee's "high-born kinsmen" bear away her body, shutting her in a sepulchre in an act of unjust interment not unlike Madeline Usher's. Unjust certainly from the point of view of the lover, the act leaves the lover behind but also "beneath" her, excluded from the "high-born" group that takes her away. The tragedy for the lover is that he remains earthbound, as the refrain "a kingdom by the sea" subtly reinforces. He is trapped *in* the world, in a geographically specific place where she was but where she is no longer.

Repetition of words and phrases emphasizes the lover's despairing sense of his "left-behindness," his inability to go "beyond." He restates the angels' covetous motive, insisting again, with an exclamatory "Yes!", that he has identified the cause of his beloved's death. The reiteration of the lover's interpretation belies his certitude, as does the parenthetical claim that this reason was valid "as all men know." Yet, the repetition also prolongs the possibility that the interpretation will be consoling to the lover. As Debra Fried has astutely discussed, repetition fosters remembrance even as it points out the futility of trying to recover the dead, serving as a fragile means of consolation that speaks intimately with the voiceless dead as well as with the reader. (See Critical Views on "The Raven.") Facing the futility of his act of remembrance, the speaker describes again a love that surpasses all human knowledge and experience. He claims that their love exceeds the power of heaven and hell, denying that either realm can "ever dissever" them. By drawing attention to the musical resonance between a word for the eternal ("ever") and the act of severing ("dissever"), Poe joins them in sound if not sense.

In the final stanza, the speaker implies that a connection has been made between the world of "beyond" and the world in which he lives. The personified moon enables a communication of sorts via dreams. The visible world reflects the body of the beloved, and the stars become her eyes. Turning from these rather conventional tropes, however, Poe concludes the poem by going deeper into the tragically earth-bound nature of the lover's obsession. In a lovely and sensuous image, the lover rejoins his beloved: "all the night-tide,

I lie down by the side / Of my darling . . . ." The lovers reconnect—not in some ethereal distance, but in the flesh, down by the sea, in the tide, in the tomb itself. The grit and reality of these final lines give the poem a chilling force. Some readers argue that "in her tomb" and "in her sepulchre" graphically reflect necrophiliac desire (see Bonaparte, below), but however literally or figuratively we interpret these lines, they create a disturbing intimacy.

Less famous but more complex and poetically interesting than "Annabel Lee," "Ulalume" (1848) shares its theme of mourning and was also likely inspired by Virginia's death. In a bizarre and vivid allegorical landscape, the speaker engages in a drama with the soul, personified as Psyche. The speaker approaches the sensual appeal of Astarte, the moon, and then confronts the burden of the memory of his dead lover. "Ulalume" is often compared with "The Bells" for the musical play Poe employs throughout, but its elusive music is more subtle and emotionally effective. The name of the lost lover, Ulalume, suggests ululation, a word of onomatopoeic origin for wailing and lamentation. Like "Annabel Lee," "Ulalume" ends with a visit to the tomb, and its haunting cadences also suggest that music mediates a condition of torturous bereavement. In both poems, the repetition of sounds at once brings solace to the grieving lover and unfolds into a song of painful communion with the deceased.

"Annabel Lee" remains popular as a timeless lament for a dark fate that comes between lovers. Whether it is considered a hymn to necrophilia or a radiant elegy, the poem exemplifies Poe's sensitivity to the melancholy and his inventive and expressive music. Striving for a musical form to approach "a love that was more than love," the poem offers a chilling look at fidelity to the memory of love, as well as a powerful meditation on beauty and death. ✾

Critical Views on
"Annabel Lee"

RUFUS GRISWOLD ON "MADNESS"

[The Rev. Rufus Griswold (1815–1857), a writer, Baptist minister, and editor of *Graham's Magazine*, was Poe's literary executor. His slanderous obituary, signed "Ludwig," and his 1850 "Memoir," damaged Poe's reputation for many years. When considering how "Annabel Lee" was read by later critics, it is important to begin with Griswold's melodramatic portrait, aware how it colored later interpretations of Poe's biography.]

He was at times a dreamer—dwelling in ideal realms—in heaven or hell, peopled with creations and the accidents of his brain. He walked the streets, in madness or melancholy, with lips moving in indistinct curses, or with eyes upturned in passionate prayers (never for himself, for he felt, or professed to feel, that he was already damned), but for their happiness who at that moment were objects of his idolatry; or with his glance introverted to a heart gnawed with anguish, and with a face shrouded in gloom, he would brave the wildest storms; and all night, with drenched garments and arms wildly beating the wind and rain, he would speak as if to spirits that at such times only could be evoked by him from that Aydin close by whose portals his disturbed soul sought to forget the ills to which his constitution subjected him—close by that Aydin where were those he loved—the Aydin which he might never see but in fitful glimpses, as its gates opened to receive the less fiery and more happy natures whose listing to sin did not involve the doom of death. He seemed, except when some fitful pursuit subjected his will and engrossed his faculties, always to bear the memory of some controlling sorrow. The remarkable poem of *The Raven* was probably much more nearly than has been supposed, even by those who were very intimate with him, a reflection and an echo of his own history. He was the bird's

> —unhappy master,
> Whom unmerciful disaster
> Followed fast and followed faster
> Till his song the burden bore—
> Melancholy burden bore
> Of "Nevermore," of "Nevermore."

Every genuine author in a greater or lesser degree leaves in his works, whatever their design, traces of his personal character; elements of his immortal being, in which the individual survives the person. While we read the pages of the *Fall of the House of Usher,* or of *Mesmeric Revelation,* we see in the solemn and stately gloom which invests one, and in the subtle metaphysical analysis of both, indications of the idiosyncracies,—of what was most peculiar—in the author's intellectual nature. But we see here only the better phases of this nature, only the symbols of his juster action, for his harsh experience had deprived him of all faith in man or woman.

—Rufus Griswold, "The 'Ludwig' Article" (New York *Daily Tribune,* October 9, 1849). Reprinted in *The Recognition of Edgar Allan Poe,* ed. Eric W. Carlson (Ann Arbor: University of Michigan Press, 1966): pp. 32–33.

Marie Bonaparte on "Necrophilia"

[A disciple of Freud, Princess Marie Bonaparte (1882–1962) published *The Life and Works of Edgar Allan Poe: A Psycho-Analytic Interpretation* in 1933. It was translated into English in 1945. Her interpretation reduces Poe's themes to universalized psychoanalytic concepts, especially the idea that he had a compulsion to repeat his grief over his mother's early death, a trauma that Virginia's death mirrored. Bonaparte reads "Annabel Lee" as expressing Poe's "repressed sado-necrophilist drives."]

Virginia's impending death was the immediate factor which occasioned the poem, but its deeper and primary source, which Virginia's condition merely reactivated, lay far back in Poe's past.

The dual contributions, from the present and past, may be seen side by side in the poem:

I was a child and she was a child. Virginia, throughout her short life, remained a child by the side of her maturer husband. But he, in infancy, had dearly loved his beautiful ailing mother, *many and many a year ago* (thus he transcribes his distant infancy), *in a kingdom by the sea*. New York, to which he had come at six months and where he lived for a year, Norfolk where, after David Poe's flight, Rosalie came into the world while Edgar was still under two, and Charleston where, in 1810 and 1822, the poor sick actress lived for six months with her two smallest children,—that is, until Edgar was two and a half—were all so many cities of that great "kingdom by the sea" where, lulled by the boom of Atlantic breakers, the little boy had loved and been loved, with a first and final all-engrossing passion.

For it was there that Edgar had loved his mother with all the intensity of the child, an intensity long forgotten by the adult, so deeply has its memory been repressed, a love none the less real for all that. . . . *"we loved with a love that was more than love—I and my Annabel Lee"*.[. . .]

This was the time when his fulfilled desires assumed and retained those "Poesque" characteristics which he derived directly from his mother; her slightness and beauty; her illness and consumption; her pallor and wasting; her blood-spittings and finally her cold, white, dead body. Poe's necrophilia, doubtless like other necrophilias the psychoanalytic study of which remains to be made, that necrophilia which Poe sublimated in art, is the supreme expression of unswerving devotion to an infantile love-object. For that reason *the moon* (a mother symbol) *never beams, without bringing me dreams/ Of the beautiful ANNABEL LEE; And the stars never rise, but I see the bright eyes/ Of the beautiful ANNABEL LEE*. These eyes, the eyes which he saw in his dreams, the eyes which were to inspire *Ligeia*, are those which, in the miniature of Elizabeth Arnold, turn their strange wide gaze upon us and were to make their adorer, Edgar, almost a fetishist of eyes.

A true necrophilist phantasy concludes the poem: *And so, all the night-tide, I lie down by the side/ Of my darling—my darling—my life and my bride,/ In her sepulchre there by the sea—/ In her tomb by the sounding sea*.

We thus see how passionately the little three-year boy would yearn to follow the mother "they" were bearing away in her strange, heavy sleep, and to sleep, as she slept, at her side. So later, at Virginia's bed, re-experiencing the dim past, he would be filled by old funereal feelings, by virtue of the repetition compulsion which governs our lives.

Annabel Lee, like Virginia, dies virgin, as in the child's unconscious phantasies of the mother, in order that none may dispute his possession of her. Meanwhile, throughout the poem, we hear the murmur of the "sounding sea", the sea so intimately wedded with Poe's infancy, the sea which, in all ages and to all men, is the universal,' phylogenetic "mother" symbol.

—Marie Bonaparte, *The Life and Works of Edgar Allan Poe: A Psycho-Analytic Interpretation*, trans. John Rodker. (London: The Hogarth Press, 1949): pp. 126–127, 130.

ALAN SHUCARD ON IMMORTAL LOVE

[Alan Shucard teaches at the University of Wisconsin, Parkside, and is the author of *Countee Cullen* (1984) and *American Poetry: The Puritans through Walt Whitman* (1988), from which this extract is taken. Shucard describes the importance of Poe's biography to understanding the portrayal of women in the poems, and offers a reading of "Annabel Lee" that elucidates the "psychic fortress" it erects.]

With Poe as with no other American poet, understanding the biography—the biographical roots of his anguish—is indispensable to understanding his conception of poetry and his poems. It is not difficult to see why he spent his artistic life seeking to change places with the angel Israfel (in the poem of that name, 1831). From "Tamerlane" (1827) on (a poem that encoded his thwarted love for Miss Royster of Richmond, and society's rejection of him), unable to contend with the physical, he cherished the spiritual; unable to fulfill relationships with flesh-and-blood women, he worshipped unearthly or even dead ones; unable to avoid his tormentor Death, he transfigured it, turned it into an object of mysterious attraction. If he tried to love a woman mortally, he could lose her, as indeed he lost them all—mothers, wife, fiancées, flirtations. But if he turned them to ether, he could worship them forever.[...]

Like Ulalume, as well as Irene, Lenore, and the unnamed lady in paradise, the object of the speaker's love in "Annabel Lee" is dead, resting in a "sepulchre there by the sea" that mirrors Poe's usual sepulchral association with the sea. And why not the sea if his representations of other natural phenomena—lakes, woods, and so on—are also sepulchral? The speaker's retreat here, though, is not really to a vaporous no-place but to a more easily recognizable psychic fortress—the human being's rationalized position of ultimate rectitude and vindication. We were better than the rest and right all the time! He values the love between himself and Annabel Lee, who is usually equated with Virginia Clemm, far above that of mortals, above the power of other mortals even to comprehend. Indeed, "the winged seraphs of Heaven/Coveted her and me" and "The angels, not half so happy in Heaven,/Wend envying her and me" because— and this is always the point in Poe's "love" poems—"we loved with a love that was more than love." In "Annabel Lee" he does not shift the relationship in space; he shifts it in kind. So intensely different is it from mere human love that it arouses the jealousy of mortals and immortals alike. Her "highborn kinsmen" bear the child-love away and "shut her up in a sepulchre," and the envy of the angels is "the reason (as all men know,/. . .) That the wind came out of the cloud, chilling/And killing my Annabel Lee." Poe's poems and tales are not wont to let death stand in the way of true unearthly love, however. His soul forever united with his lover's, the speaker lies down with her "all the night-tide.../In her sepulchre there by the sea—/In her tomb by the side of the sea."

—Alan Shucard, *American Poetry: The Puritans through Walt Whitman* (Boston: Twayne, 1988): pp. 114, 118.

JOAN DAYAN ON POE AND THE FEMININE

[Joan Dayan, Professor of English and African-American studies at the University of Arizona, is the author of *Fables of Mind: An Inquiry into Poe's Fiction* (1987) and *Haiti, History, and the Gods* (1995). In this extract, Dayan interrogates Poe's "feminine" style and his images of violated women as both undermining and reinforcing gendered paradigms.]

Poe's poetry is a rite of the image. If it is "woman" in nineteenth-century America who must bear the trappings of style, Poe shows, by assuming a lady's style and postures, how such a spectacle both exploits and consumes its participants. Taking Luce Irigaray in *This Sex Which Is Not One* as our medium here, let us say that Poe's generalizations, his totalizing images are ways of "'re-opening' the figures of philosophical discourse—idea, substance, subject, transcendental subjectivity, absolute knowledge—in order to pry out of them what they have borrowed that is feminine, to make them 'render up' and give back what they owe the feminine." There is a two-way program here. On one hand, Poe plays with the possibility of one thing passing into another and vice versa—the *controvertibility* that is so much a part of his project to annihilate innate principles. On the other hand, since a man performs the ungendering operation, or the project of *indifference,* the writing subject Mr. Poe appropriates and replays the attributes of women projected in his society. He dramatizes this appropriation in order to expose and overturn all gestures of idealization. When Poe fights to make physical and spiritual mutually adaptable—as in the poems we have discussed, in *Eureka,* and in many of his tales—he destroys the gap between what is perceptible and what is intelligible in order to take further his analysis of subordination by gender.[...]

But what are we to do with Poe's bleeding, raped, decapitated, dead, and resurrected women, brutalized, buried, cemented in cellars, and stuffed up chimneys? No matter where you turn in the tales, women—and their bodies (or sex as in "The Oblong Box")—remain crucial to Poe's tools of terror. Scenes of violation and Poe's indomitable "imp of the perverse" depend on women for their effect. So, characterizations of women as "innocent," "angelic" or "evil," "beauties" or "hags"—the traditional stereotypes—become useless in interpreting Poe's fiction. Whether Dupin's quest to know *who done it,* or a pathological attempt to get into a room ("The Tell-Tale Heart"), or the discovery of a "rotted, erect" wife ("The Premature Burial"), Poe is after nothing less than an exhumation of the lived, but disavowed or suppressed experiences of women in his society. Demonstrating how the terms for denigration or praise are themselves covers for an experience of subjugation shared by both "ladies" and "wenches," he lays bare the mechanics of cultural control in the Anglo-American experience.[...]

The destruction or death of Poe's women is never final, as shown in the haunting bodily returns of Lady Madeline, Ligeia, or Morella. Other women mark his fiction in less obvious, but equally significant ways. Even though Poe destroys the idea of femininity, pulverizing something called "purity" in loathsome physical dismemberments, women's sexed bodies remain. . . .To know an answer for these narrators demands a re-physicalizing of what their culture had spiritualized, giving blood to the beautiful illusion, and contaminating those "angels in the house."

—Joan Dayan, "Poe's Women: A Feminist Poe?" *Poe Studies* 26, nos. 1–2 (June-December 1993): pp. 9, 10, 11.

⊛

Monika Elbert on the Maternal Gothic

[Monika Elbert teaches at Montclair State College and is the author of several articles on the Gothic and maternity in American literature, including work on Edith Wharton and Nathaniel Hawthorne. In this essay, employing the insights of French feminist theory, Elbert offers a very different psychoanalytic interpretation of "Annabel Lee" than Bonaparte does, describing Poe's "maternal landscapes" and his desire "to capture and appropriate the mother tongue."]

Poe, in his numerous stories of the mother or variations of the mother figure, tries so hard to be in control of feeling through the language of logic or Logos that he inevitably lapses back into the womb/tomb of the mother—the realm of the unutterable, the unmentionable—into, as Carolyn Burke describes Kristeva's maternal semiotics, "gaps in meaning, pauses, and silences," which, for French feminist Julia Kristeva, represent "a body-to-body discourse with the mother." It is not so much the Oedipal/sexual connection to the mother as it is an irretrievable non-linguistic connection to her which fascinates Poe. He longs for the incubatory state (which Julia Kristeva would consider the semiotic realm), the preverbal realm of experience in the womb and prior to knowledge of the father's limiting symbolic language (in Lacanian terms, the "nom [non] du pere"). Poe recreates his world through recreating the pre-Oedipal period of connection between mother and child, which is at the heart of feminine language, according to Kristeva. Many of Poe's poems and short stories dealing with women try to recreate the mother whose language he cannot decipher, whose soul he cannot penetrate. Yet, she remains for him the source of imagination and meditation, as for example, when he associates Annabel Lee's life-giving force with the tomb/sea, which resonates in the reader's mind as womb.[...]

Poe's attempt to possess the mother tongue is connected to the Gothic genre of his tales. Poe's Gothic houses of horror are not so much emblems of the mind as they are symbols of repressed maternal semiotics. In French feminist Luce Irigaray's terms, male fantasies portray the mother as a container which he wants to possess: he fears her true nature as "open container" or fluidy realm; "man needs to represent her as a *closed* volume, a container; his desire is to immobilize her, keep her under his control, in his possession, even in his house. For Poe, it is a desire to capture and appropriate the mother tongue—hence the imprisoned women/mothers of his Gothic mansions. Poe's maternal landscapes or mere/mer/nightmare-scapes are always tinged with the Gothic— what Eve Kosofsky Sedgwick says of the Gothic novel holds true for Poe's tales: "[T]he male paranoid plot is not separate from the maternal or monstrous plot; instead there is articulated within the text a male paranoid *reading* of maternity, a reading that persistently renders uncanny, renders as violence of a particular kind, the coming-to-body of the (male) individual subject." In Poe, this (literal) coming to life of the male or his enlightenment always entails the death of the mother so that birth and death are inextricably bound. Julia Kristeva links the Freudian death drive with maternal origins and ultimately with matricide: "[T]he unrepresentable nature of death was linked with that other unrepresentable—original abode but also last resting place for dead souls, in the beyond— which, for mythical thought, is constituted by the female body."

—Monika Elbert, "Poe's Gothic Mother and the Incubation of Language," *Poe Studies* 26, nos. 1–2 (June-December 1993): pp. 23–24.

Works by
Edgar Allan Poe

Tamerlane and Other Poems. (1827).

El Aaraaf, Tamerlane and Minor Poems. (1829).

Poems, Second Edition. (1831).

The Narrative of Arthur Gordon Pym. (1838).

The Conchologist's First Book. (1839).

Tales of the Grotesque and Arabesque. (1840).

The Prose Romances of Edgar A. Poe. (1843).

The Raven and Other Poems. (1845).

Tales. (1845).

Eureka: A Prose Poem. (1848).

Works about
Edgar Allan Poe

Alexander, Jean. *Affidavits of Genius: Edgar Allan Poe and the French Critics, 1847–1924.* Port Washington, NY: Kennikat Press, 1971.

Allen, Michael. *Poe and the Magazine Tradition.* New York: Oxford University Press, 1969.

Auden, W. H. "Introduction." *Edgar Allan Poe: Selected Prose and Poetry.* New York: Rinehart, 1950.

Baudelaire, Charles. *Baudelaire on Poe.* Trans. and ed. Lois and Francis E. Hyslop, Jr. State College, PA: Bald Eagle Press, 1952.

Bloom, Harold. "The Inescapable Poe." *New York Review of Books* 31, no. 15 (Oct. 11, 1984).

Bonaparte, Marie. *Edgar Poe: Sa vie, son oeuvre—Étude psychanalytique.* Paris: Denoel et Steele, 1933. Trans. John Rodker. *The Life and Works of Edgar Allan Poe: A Psycho-Analytic Interpretation.* London: Imago, 1949.

Buranelli, Vincent. *Edgar Allan Poe.* New York: Twayne, 1961.

Campbell, Killis. *The Mind of Poe and Other Studies.* Cambridge: Harvard University Press, 1933.

———, ed. *The Poems of Edgar Allan Poe.* New York: Ginn, 1917.

Caputi, Anthony. "The Refrain in Poe's Poetry." *AL* 25 (1953): 160–73.

Carlson, Eric W., ed. *A Companion to Poe Studies.* Westport, CT: Greenwood Press, 1996.

———. *Critical Essays on Edgar Allan Poe.* Boston: Hall, 1987.

———. *The Recognition of Edgar Allan Poe: Selected Criticism Since 1829.* Ann Arbor: University of Michigan Press, 1966.

Davidson, Edward. *Poe: A Critical Study.* Cambridge: Harvard University Press, 1957.

Dayan, Joan. "From Romance to Modernity: Poe and the Work of Poetry." *Studies in Romanticism* 29 (1990): 413–438.

———. "Poe's Women: A Feminist Poe?" *Poe Studies* 26 (1993): 1–12.

Elbert, Monika. "Poe's Gothic Mother and the Incubation of Language." *Poe Studies* 26 (1993): 22–33.

Eliot, T. S. "From Poe to Valéry" (1948). In *To Criticize the Critic.* New York: Farrar, Straus and Giroux, 1980, 27–42.

Fisher, Benjamin Franklin, IV. "Fantasy Figures in Poe's Poems." *The Poetic Fantastic: Studies in an Evolving Genre.* New York: Greenwood Press, 1989, 43–51.

————, ed. and introd. *Poe and His Times: The Artist and His Milieu.* Baltimore: Edgar Allan Poe Society, 1990.

Fried, Debra. "Repetition, Refrain, and Epitaph." *ELH* 53 (1986): 615–32.

Hoffman, Daniel. *Poe Poe Poe Poe Poe Poe Poe.* New York: Doubleday, 1972.

Irwin, John T. *American Hieroglyphics: The Symbol of the Egyptian Hieroglyphics in the American Renaissance.* New Haven: Yale University Press, 1980.

Jacobs, Robert D. *Poe: Journalist and Critic.* Baton Rouge: Louisiana State Universtiy Press, 1969.

Krutch, Joseph W. *Edgar Allan Poe: A Study in Genius.* New York: Russell and Russell, 1926.

Lawrence, D. H. "Edgar Allan Poe." *Studies in Classic American Literature.* First published 1923. New York: Penguin, 1977, 83–88.

Mabbott, Thomas Ollive, ed. *Collected Works of Edgar Allan Poe, I: Poems.* Cambridge, Harvard University Press, 1969.

Meyers, Jeffrey. "Edgar Allan Poe." *The Columbia History of American Poetry.* ed. Jay Parini. New York: Columbia University Press, 1993, 172–202.

————. *Edgar Allan Poe: Life and Legacy.* New York: Macmillan, 1992.

Person, Leland. "Poe's Composition of Philosophy: Reading and Writing 'The Raven.'" *Arizona Quarterly* 46 (1990): 1–15.

Phillips, Elizabeth. "The Poems: 1824–1835." *A Companion to Poe Studies.* Ed. Eric W. Carlson. Westport, CT: Greenwood Press, 1996, 67–88.

Quinn, Patrick F. *The French Face of Edgar Poe.* Carbondale: Southern Illinois University Press, 1957.

Smith, Dave. "Edgar Allan Poe and the Nightmare Ode." *Southern Humanities Review* 29 (1995): 1–10.

Smith, Grover. "Eliot and the Ghost of Poe." *T. S. Eliot: A Voice Descanting.* Ed. Shyamal Bagchee. New York: St. Martin's Press, 1990, 149–63.

Stovall, Floyd. *Edgar Poe the Poet.* Charlottesville: University Press of Virginia, 1969.

————, ed. *The Poems of Edgar Allan Poe.* Charlottesville: University Press of Virginia, 1965.

Tate, Allen. "Our Cousin, Mr. Poe." *Collected Essays.* Denver: Alan Swallow, 1959.

————. "The Poetry of Edgar Allan Poe." *Sewanee Review* 76 (1968): 214–25.

Thorpe, Dwayne. "The Poems: 1836–1849." *A Companion to Poe Studies.* Ed. Eric W. Carlson. Westport, CT: Greenwood Press, 1996, 89–109.

Vines, Lois Davis. *Valéry and Poe: A Literary Legacy.* New York: New York University Press, 1992.

Wilbur, Richard. *Responses; Prose Pieces, 1953–1976.* New York: Harcourt Brace Jovanovich, 1976. Reprints of three essays on Poe.

Williams, W. C. "Edgar Allan Poe." *In the American Grain.* New York: New Directions, 1925.

Winters, Yvor. "Edgar Allan Poe: A Crisis in the History of American Obscurantism." *American Literature* 8 (Jan. 1937): 379–401.

Index of
Themes and Ideas

"AL AARAAF," 31

"ANNABEL LEE," 9, 73–84; acoustical effects of language in, 75, 76; as ballad, 74; critical views on, 77–84; immortal love in, 80–81; meter of, 74; necrophilia in, 76, 78–80; Poe's biography and, 77–81; purity and ideality in, 74; repetition in, 74, 75, 76; as response to deaths of "beautiful women," 73, 80–81; rhythm of, 74; supernatural in, 74–75; thematic analysis of, 73–76; "Ulalume" and, 76; Virginia's death in, 73, 78–80, 81

"BELLS, THE," 9, 63–72; acoustic effects of language in, 63–65, 66–67; critical views on, 66–72; meaning from music in, 64–65, 71–72; melodrama in, 65; mourning in, 65; repetition in, 63, 64; rhythm in, 63, 64, 65; thematic analysis of, 63–65; "Ulalume" and, 76

"CITY IN THE SEA, THE," 14–31; acoustic value of words in, 16–17; as allegory, 16; beauty in, 26; critical views on, 18–31; death-obsession in, 14, 15; difficulty of envisioning city in, 15–16, 25–26; God in, 16; Hell in, 16; imagery in, 15, 17, 25–26, 27; influences on, 14–15; meter in, 16; obscurity in, 26; otherworldly panorama of, 15; psychological-artistic interpretation of, 25–26; rhyme in, 16; sources of city in, 14, 26–28; stasis and movement in, 16; symbols of civilization in, 15; thematic analysis of, 14–17; thematic and moral significance of, 15–16; water in, 15; world in post-apocalyptic state in, 14, 17

"COLISEUM, THE," 31

"DREAM-LAND," 9

"EUREKA," 13, 29, 30, 66, 82

"HAUNTED PALACE, THE," 32–45; as allegory, 33; Baudelaire and, 36–37; critical views on, 36–45; desolation in, 33–34; house as head in, 32; imagery of, 32; language in, 34–35; narrator of, 32; nostalgia in, 33; primordial perversity of, 36–37; sleep-consciousness in, 37–39; spatial analogy in, 41–42; symbols of, 33; thematic analysis of, 32–35; transformation in, 37–39; unraveling of sanity in, 42–43; Madeline Usher in, 32–33, 34; Roderick Usher in, 32–33, 34, 35, 38–39, 43

"I SAW THEE ON THY BRIDAL DAY," 31

"ON THE MATERIAL AND SPIRITUAL UNIVERSE," 13

"PHILOSOPHY OF COMPOSITION, THE," 23, 54, 55–56, 58–59, 60, 61

POE, EDGAR ALLAN: aesthetic inadequacies of, 9–10, 11; allegory and, 70; Baudelaire and, 36–37, 40; beauty as object of poetry of, 13, 18–20, 24, 29, 63; biography of, 11–13, 73, 77–81; Byron and, 14–15, 39; Coleridge and, 14, 46, 47, 74; as craftsman, 69–70; early poems of, 30–31; Eliot and, 44–45; feminine style of, 81–83; hysteria and, 10, 11; infinity and, 41–42; Keats and, 14, 46; Mallarmé and, 40; maternal Gothic and, 83–84; as melancholy, 77–78; meter of, 22; musical effect in poems of, 66–67; obscurity of, 21–22; originality of, 21–22; perfectionism of, 31; permanent popularity of, 9–10, 11; range of styles of, 30–31; rhythm of, 22; Shelley and, 39, 46; subjects of, 24; as transitional figure, 28–30; unearthly visions of, 23–24; Valéry and, 40; Whitman on character of, 19–20; word play of, 67–69

"POETIC PRINCIPLE, THE," 13, 18–19, 29, 63

"RAVEN, THE," 9, 13, 46–62; artificiality in, 54; as autobiographical, 77; as bad poem, 60–62; critical views on, 50–62; experimentation in, 53–54; horror fantasy in, 56–58; Lenore in, 47, 48, 62; literary antecedents for, 46; melancholy tone of, 46, 48, 50, 51; as melodrama, 61; meter of, 22, 46, 47, 54; originality of, 22; "The Philosophy of Composition" and, 54, 55–56, 58–59, 60, 61; phraseology of, 52; Poe on, 50–51; problem of interpretation of, 47, 48–49; psychological derangement and, 49, 56–58, 61; repetition in, 47, 49, 55–56; rhythm of, 22, 46, 52, 53; self-deconstruction in, 58–60; South and, 61–62; speaker in, 47–49, 54, 56–58; thematic analysis of, 46–49; as triumph of imagination and art, 51–53

"ROSE AYLMER," 22

"SLEEPER, THE," 22

"TAMERLANE," 80

"ULALUME," 9, 22, 76